THE REJECTED STONE

AL SHARPTON AND THE PATH
TO AMERICAN LEADERSHIP

REVEREND AL SHARPTON

WITH NICK CHILES

CASH MONEY CONTENT

MASSENBURG
▶media

First Hardcover Edition: October 2013

Book Layout: Peng Olaguera/ISPN

Cover Design: Michael Nagin

Cover Photography: Deborah Feingold

www.CashMoneyContent.com

Library of Congress Control Number: 2013942088

ISBN: 978-1-936399-47-5 hc

ISBN: 978-1-936399-48-2 ebook

10 9 8 7 6 5 4 3 2 1

Printed in the United States

CONTENTS

CONTENTS

*I dedicate this book to the three anchors of my life,
who, incidentally, are the three women after
whom I have molded my life thus far.*

A

ADA SHARPTON

*My mother was the foundation of my life and taught me values
and self-confidence and sacrificed everything, even after she
had lost everything. She worked to make me something that
I hope she was proud of before she passed in March 2012.*

D

DOMINIQUE SHARPTON

*My older child is a gifted artist and a passionate activist
in her own right. I not only love but cherish her commitment
to the things that I believe in and her commitment in her
own right to making that legacy live on.*

A

ASHLEY SHARPTON

*My younger child has a genius ability to create
and the discipline to execute whatever she sets out
to do, with a tenacity that reminds me of myself.*

These three ladies—my past, my present, and my future—
make this book possible because there would not have
been a story or author to write it without this trio.

THE REJECTED STONE

1

CHANGING WITH THE TIMES—
MY UNLIKELY JOURNEY

On January 21, 2013, shortly before noon, with my heart pounding in my chest, I saw five decades of my political and activist life pass before my eyes.

As I walked down the long, carpeted trail in the ornate United States Capitol Building, toward the inauguration stage, where I would join other luminaries, celebrities, close friends, and family members of Barack Obama to watch him—along with millions viewing on TV—be sworn in for his second term as the president of the United States, I thought about how unlikely the entire day was.

I thought about the journey my country had traversed in my lifetime, from establishing the right to vote for African-Americans with the 1965 Voting Rights Act when I was just nine years old to the second inauguration of a black man as president when I was fifty-eight.

I thought about my mother, Ada Sharpton, who raised my sister and me by herself and had died the previous year.

I thought about the guys who went to school with me in Brooklyn. Some of them were dead, some were in jail, and some were trapped in the endless cycle of drugs. None of them thought we would ever amount to anything. Yet I had been able to break out of the hood in Brownsville, and here I was, walking down the steps in the Capitol behind Supreme Court justices. I wondered if any of those kids who had laughed at me, the boy preacher, were watching me now.

I thought about all my critics through the years: those racists who threw watermelons at me when I marched through Bensonhurst; those in the media and beyond who ridiculed me when I defended Tawana Brawley; those in law enforcement who wanted to prosecute me through the years, saying I was nothing but a hustler.

No one could have predicted this outcome when I was marching in Howard Beach or when I was handcuffed to a barge in Vieques, Puerto Rico, or when I was sitting in the visitors' room at the federal jail in Brooklyn during my three-month sentence. Who could have figured I'd one day be sitting across from the attorney general of the United States?

I had gotten up at four thirty A.M. to meet the other guests of the president at a hotel, where we were put on private buses and driven to St. John's Episcopal Church, a small church across the street from the White House. It was tradition for every president to begin his inauguration day with a service at St. John's. I was among 250 guests who had been invited to join the president, the vice president, and their families for the church service that morning.

I sat in the third row on the right side of the church. As many pulpits and churches as I've been in down through the years—literally thousands—this one felt different. Because this time, the only way you could get there was to be invited by the president of the United States. As I listened to the ministers and the songs that morning, I looked over at the president, this man who sat there with the burdens of the world on his shoulders, this man who had gotten there because of the sacrifices of many who had fought and even died during the nation's ugly battles over equality and civil rights. I looked around the congregation and saw the secretary of defense, the secretary of state, people who controlled the military-industrial complex. Sitting among them were people like me and Martin Luther King III, people who had come out of the freedom movement. Although we were not veterans of wars, we were veterans of battles. We were scarred not by warfare but from the handcuffs and the media attacks, the false investigations and the merciless and reckless allegations.

As we left that church, I stopped and met Elie Wiesel, the Nobel laureate who had survived the Holocaust camps in Nazi Germany. I thought about how there currently were and had been battles fought all over the world for human rights, whether against the Nazis, against apartheid, against slavery and segregation, against Northern racists. And I knew that while it was impressive to meet the heads of state and commerce, the freedom fighters like Wiesel and Martin III and others who joined us that morning were the people I most admired. Because I knew that, like me, they had had periods in their lives when they were not exactly warmly embraced in the corridors of power, when they might even have been considered pariahs. They were there because someone had recognized the value in their struggles. They weren't there just because it was inaugural protocol, the thing to do on Inauguration Day.

When we walked down those final steps in the chute and then stepped out onto the open stage, we appeared on the big screen. I could hear applause. As I looked out among the throng and heard the clapping, I imagined it was coming from the folks who knew how unlikely it was to see me up there, with my James Brown hairdo.

One hundred forty pounds lighter.

The medallion I used to wear long gone.

As were the sweat suits that used to be my uniform, worn in the style of my contemporaries such as Run-D.M.C.

Now I had on a tailored suit. I had on a tie. But I was still Reverend Al from Brownsville. I was there representing all the unlikelies out there. I was there for the rejects. I was there for the people who others thought would never amount to anything.

But I went to that inauguration stage on my own terms. I never sold out my principles. I never backed down from what I believed. I never apologized for standing up. I never regretted going to jail and marching. It is one thing to beat the odds and achieve something as you transform, but it's another thing not to have to do it at the expense of your own soul. Because you can grow, but you don't have to break. You can have the courage to change without having to compromise your basic integrity.

As I walked down those steps and took my seat, picking up the blue blanket that said "Honored guest of the President of the United States," I knew that everybody watching at home—and those who were not watching—has an opportunity to transform as I did. To transform as American society has transformed. Because underlying my reflections about the distance of my own journey was the knowledge that American society had also undergone a startling transformation over those years. This was reflected most of all in the basic reason for my presence on that stage: A black man, a friend of mine, was being sworn in as president of the United States. And a Puerto Rican woman was swearing in the vice president.

Neither one of those facts would have been possible in the early days of my career. As America changed, grew more tolerant and more accepting, it allowed people like me to change my tactics. I no longer had to be as confrontational to get an audience. I no longer had to be as radical to make the authorities pay attention. The country grew and, in the process, allowed me to grow.

As I prepared to take my seat, I felt someone tap me on the shoulder. I turned around and was greeted by Jay-Z and Beyoncé. They were there because Beyoncé was to sing the national anthem. Jay-Z came from the same streets of Brooklyn that I did. This guy who had hustled on the streets, selling dope—how unlikely was it for him to be on that stage? But there he was, a music mogul, a multimillionaire, a cultural trendsetter. He and I, two kids from Brooklyn, a half-generation apart, sitting on that platform together, the ultimate examples of the fact that any of us can truly be what we want if we're not afraid to grow into our ultimate destiny.

After I sat down, I looked across the aisle at Clarence Thomas. He stood for everything I despised, but he was sitting there in the black robe of the Supreme Court, a black boy born and raised in the segregationist South. How unlikely was it that this man, who grew up as a hated target of Jim Crow's wrath, would don that black robe?

I sat on the platform among people who represented American power, but all of them were unlikely in their own way, from Vice President Joe Biden to House Speaker John Boehner, from Michelle Obama to Supreme Court Justice Sonia Sotomayor. But while I didn't know all the details of their stories, their paths, I knew my own. And I knew there were many people who would find my presence on that stage unbelievable. But I didn't. All that I was I always believed I would be. I believed what the Bible said, that the rejected stones would become the cornerstones of a new world order. Race and class and gender bias and homophobia were all on their deathbed, on the verge of being swept into the dustbins of history.

As Barack Hussein Obama, the forty-fourth president of the United States, put his hand on that Bible, I put my hand on my mental Bible. While he took his oath of office, I took my own special oath. My oath said that as the world continues to change, we all must remember that, as Gandhi said, change starts by changing yourself. And I will be committed throughout the rest of my life to spreading change, fighting for transformation, battling for the rejected stones, trying with all my might to remain a walking billboard with a simple message: Never let your environment and your circumstances limit your possibilities.

As you read through the following pages and get a sense of my journey and the lessons I've learned, I believe you will come to understand why I've not been unsettled or slowed down by the attempts over the years to paint me with a broad brush as some kind of troublemaker or self-interested hustler. While those caricatures might have become media shorthand, I was not about to let the world define me. This is one of the most important lessons I've learned over the years: Even if everyone around you thinks you're wrong, you must have the strength to stand strong for what you believe in. You must do this with some honesty and some humility—to be able to look at yourself and admit the areas where you are weak and where you are strong, where you could have done better, where you came up short. And, crucially, you must not be afraid to grow with the times.

The America I faced in the 1980s wearing my jogging suit was not the same place as the America I speak to now, yet I still find myself leading marches to protest outrages such as the shooting death of Trayvon Martin or the widespread attempts to roll back voting rights. I moved with the times, updating my style and my approach so that I never became irrelevant. If you do it right, as I hope I did, you can become part of the reason the times they are a-changin'.

2

IF YOU WANT TO LEAD, YOU MUST DECIDE WHERE YOU'RE GOING

One of the early things I learned about leadership—about transforming yourself into someone whom others will follow—is how intentional it is. Most of the great leaders don't get there by accident, suddenly waking up one morning to find greatness patiently waiting on their front stoop. No, there's careful and strategic planning at work from very early in their lives. Deliberating. Reading. Researching. Sometimes there may be a bit of luck and the guiding hand of others helping along the way; it doesn't usually happen in isolation, without input and mentorship.

I've had many opportunities over the years to go off in different directions, whether it was to become the head of some big megachurch or to spend my life living fabulously on the road with James Brown, but that wasn't what I had in mind for Alfred Sharpton. I knew I wanted to be a civil rights activist, so I began to take the steps in that direction before I had even reached my tenth birthday.

I tell young people that you can't arrive someplace until you determine the destination. It sounds simple, almost clichéd, but it's an inescapable truth. If I'm at the airport, I can't buy a ticket until I know where I'm going. That's the first thing they ask you when you step up to the counter. Next, you have to deal with the cost—this is the price of your trip, so are you willing to pay the price to get there? That's something every potential leader has to decide: Is it worth it to me to wake up at four A.M. every day and run around the park like Muhammad Ali training for a fight or to stay in the recording studio all night to get it right like James Brown? The price of leadership may be graduating from Harvard Law School and going into the projects of Chicago to work for peanuts, like a young Barack Obama. Or it may be taking an Oxford and a Yale Law School education and going to Newark, New Jersey, to live in the slums and be a community organizer like the young Cory Booker. In my case, it was turning my back on the life of a megachurch pastor, with all of its material benefits, to spend the next thirty years picketing and going to jail.

What is your intention for your life, and are you willing to pay the price to get there? The destination determines the cost; the cost never determines the destination. You can't look for the cheap shortcuts to greatness—it doesn't work that way.

After that airport ticket taker finds out your destination and tells you the cost, what do they ask for next? Your ID. Who are you? Do you have the character to get to your destination?

My early years were a perfect illustration of this: I grew up deep in the hood, surrounded by all the temptations and traps that come in such an environment, yet I walked around in elementary and middle school telling the other kids and the teachers that I was going to be a preacher. Can you imagine how much teasing and abuse I had to endure? I couldn't go to the same parties as my classmates, I couldn't hang out with the same girls as my classmates, I couldn't have the same habits as my classmates. I'm the same age as all of them, part of the same culture, living in the same community, immersed in the same environment, but my ID said something different from theirs, based on my destination. And I could never forget that.

Once I decided I wanted to preach, I became obsessive. I would listen closely to every great preacher who came through my home church, Washington Temple Church of God in Christ. It was one of the biggest churches in New York, so everybody visited at some point, like Mahalia Jackson, with whom I would later tour, and Dr. Martin Luther King Jr., whom I met twice when I was just a kid. I would buy albums and listen to all the great preachers, such as Rev. William Holmes Borders and Rev. C. L. Franklin, Aretha Franklin's daddy. I was a sponge, absorbing everything I could, picking up little nuances that I thought I could incorporate into my own preaching. Around this time, I noticed that I was increasingly drawn to social justice. My pastor, Bishop F. D. Washington, would openly tell people, "I raised that boy to be the head of our denomination." But it became clear to me that's not who I wanted to be. I wanted to be Dr. Martin Luther King or Rev. Jesse Jackson or

Rep. Adam Clayton Powell Jr., men who were called to serve both God and their people through activism.

I dived into learning about civil rights leaders just as I had dived into learning about the preachers. There was nothing Jesse wrote that I didn't have a copy of, nothing James Farmer, who was in the Congress of Racial Equality (CORE), did that I hadn't heard about. I knew their styles, knew their rhythms. Methodically, obsessively, I tried to take in everything I could. Some kids wanted to be athletes and knew every tiny detail of Willie Mays's life. I knew everything about Jesse Jackson and James Farmer and MLK. While my classmates were outside playing ball, I was inside reading King's *Where Do We Go from Here?* This need to preach and serve wasn't something imposed on me; it just bubbled up from within, something I attached to on my own. I had no guarantees I would find a life there, never mind a livelihood. But I knew that was where I wanted to be.

My mother recognized my yearning at an early age and did whatever she could to encourage it. When my family moved to a big house in Queens, she built me a little chapel in the basement, complete with three or four benches for pews and a little stage that was the pulpit. While the other kids in Hollis were outside playing punchball and stickball in the streets, I would go down to the basement and preach, lining up my sister's dolls on the pews to act as my congregation. It felt like the most natural thing in the world to me at the time, though it might have looked a bit strange to outsiders. And no amount of ridicule or other kids calling me weird mattered to me, because I knew what I wanted to do, where I felt the most at home. In fact, the more I was teased or encouraged to do other things, the more it made me want to preach.

As I got older, I continued to encounter pressures to do other things, and I continued stubbornly to say no. When I ran for mayor of New York in 1997 and just missed forcing Ruth Messinger into a runoff, I got an interesting visit at my home in Brooklyn by three New York luminaries. Former mayor David Dinkins, Congressman Charlie Rangel and former Manhattan borough president and business mogul Percy Sutton sat me down and tried to get me to run for Congress. They wanted me to take on Rep. Ed Towns, a Brooklyn congressman who had broken with the Democratic establishment and endorsed Republican Mayor Rudy Giuliani for reelection. Because I had won the borough of Brooklyn in the mayoral primary, they thought I'd have an easy time beating Towns. I told them I would think about it; for weeks, they continued to lobby me to run. But ultimately, I decided I couldn't do it. Some of my detractors said I didn't want to hold office and be held accountable; my friends were telling me I could be New York's star congressman. But the reason I said no was simple: I didn't want to be a congressman.

When you are being pushed into something by others, you have to look inward and ask yourself: Do I really want to do this? Will I be at peace with myself if I say yes? I wanted to be what I had become, a national civil rights leader and an advocate using the media to push important causes. If I had gone to Congress, I don't know if we would have been able to pass racial-profiling laws; I wouldn't have been able to move around the country trying to protect voting rights; I wouldn't have been able to march on behalf of all those who had been unjustly slain, such as Trayvon Martin. And I would have been miserable, because I would have been outside of my mission, away from my passion.

Whatever your politics, you must find your comfort zone. And stick with it. Don't let other people talk you into what seems to be a more appealing or lucrative career if it doesn't match your purpose in life. If you succumb to the allure of money or prestige, the rewards will never be enough if it isn't your passion.

3

BREAKING THE SHACKLES
OF CHILDHOOD

My father abandoning my family when I was nine was one of the most devastating and consequential events of my childhood. It also instilled in me a desire to break the generational curse of father abandonment that haunts so many families, particularly in the African-American community. Once my own daughters were born, I vowed to do everything in my power to remain a strong and influential presence in their lives, no matter what.

This is a lesson that all of us from "broken" homes need to carry out of our childhoods: Don't allow the shackles of a challenging childhood hold you down.

Until the age of nine, I lived in a stable, middle-class, two-parent household in Hollis, Queens. My father had plumbing and construction companies, and he owned several pieces of property. He bought himself and my mother new late-model

15

Cadillacs every year, which they parked in the garage connected to our house. It was the epitome of 1950s idyllic suburban life. I was happy. But it all ended when I was nine and my dad ran off with my mother's oldest daughter from her previous marriage—in other words, his teenage stepdaughter. One day he was there, the next day he was gone. I didn't understand the gravity of the incest, but I knew that his act instantly transformed my life and traumatized our entire family. My world flipped overnight. The whole ordeal almost gave my mother a nervous breakdown, and it cast me out on a lifelong journey to fill the hole he left in my heart and to search for men who could act as stand-ins for the father I no longer had.

For several months, my mother, my sister, and I lived in a house with no electricity or gas because my mother had no money. When she lost the house, we ended up moving to Brooklyn and living the typically grueling existence of the hard-core ghetto: welfare, food stamps, housing projects, single motherhood. This was 1963, so sociologists such as William Julius Wilson hadn't yet applied their analytical microscopes to black poverty, but this part of Brownsville, Brooklyn, was the classic portrait of what sociologists would later call a "disadvantaged" neighborhood. They were difficult days. What made it worse for me was knowing that part of my mother's struggle was to figure out how to get me a couple of suits for my growing body so that I had something nice to wear to my preaching jobs.

The shock of my life changing so severely and drastically surely did some long-lasting damage to my psyche, but when I look back on it now, I think the most damaging aspect of it all was the raw, aching sense of abandonment I felt. My father just walked out of my life. It would be nearly four decades before we would reconnect. The abandonment was made worse by the fact that he had my older sister, Cheryl, the first child he had with my mother, come and live with him and his new wife for a while, leaving me behind in Brooklyn. I was named after him; I looked like him. But I distinctly remember feeling as if my father didn't want me. It was incredibly debilitating. I was a nine-year-old boy without an anchor, unmoored in this new world. So I reached desperately for any father figure I could find, a replacement that could help fill the emptiness that ate away at my insides. I found a lot of what I was looking for in the church.

My preaching career started at the age of four, when Bishop Washington allowed me to stand on a box at the pulpit and ser-monize to a congregation of 900 people on the anniversary of the Junior Usher Board. When I started to become known in the community as the boy preacher, it was not looked on kindly by my classmates. Their reaction ranged from outrage to amuse-ment, with a bit of everything in between. I never got beaten up, but they clearly thought I was a strange kid. They were either laughing at me or trying to avoid me. It wasn't helped by my insistence in writing "Rev. Alfred Sharpton" at the top of my papers in school, which upset my teachers so much for some reason that my mother had to come to school to inter-vene. It was my first real confrontation with authority, but it was also affirming for me, my insistence that I was *something*, someone of worth, despite the rejection by my father, despite the craziness that my life had become. My growing identity as a boy preacher undoubtedly helped my self-esteem at the time, but it also increased the sense of isolation I was feeling. It put me further out of step with my contemporaries, made me an oddity. After all, I was their mothers' preacher on Sunday. How were they supposed to act toward me on Monday?

Bishop Washington took me under his wing, with the intent of nurturing and guiding me so that one day I could succeed him as pastor of the church and maybe even become a bishop in the Church of God in Christ. I began to do the circuit, preaching at different churches in the area. That's when I went on the road at the age of nine with Mahalia Jackson, traveling with the most famous gospel singer in the world as her opening act, as the astounding boy preacher from Brooklyn. I knew Mahalia was huge, but I had been preaching for so many years already that this became second nature to me. One of my distinct memories from that period was opening for Mahalia at the 1964 World's Fair, at the circular pavilion and replica of the globe—the Unisphere—in Queens, that you can still see when you fly into LaGuardia, next to the USTA Billie Jean King National Tennis Center where the U.S. Open is held. This made a serious impression on my classmates. So what was at first odd and amusing soon became a reason to hold me in a certain amount of esteem, or at least respect. They'd point to me, saying, "There's the boy preacher." But no more "Ha ha ha" to go along with it. Opening for Mahalia Jackson at age nine will do that for you.

Just because I was the boy preacher didn't mean that I wanted to be isolated from my peers, but that's what happened. If I went outside to play punchball, guys would play with me, but I could tell they really didn't want to. And as for the girls? They found it all extremely weird. How are you going to do naughty things with a preacher? I was a rigid fundamentalist Christian, but I was still a growing boy moving into adolescence and puberty, with an escalating interest in girls. And no outlet for that interest. And the adults around me either exalted me or admonished me because they were holding me to an entirely different standard than my peers. In the middle of all that, I was still seeking a father figure. So it was a big, messy stew of difficult emotions I was grappling with at the time.

When I got older and had children of my own, I realized that I had no road map to follow, no role model to help me figure out how to do this thing called fatherhood. But I quickly realized that maybe the most important element of fatherhood was to be a bedrock for my children, to be there always as a support system for them—all the things my father never was for me. When my wife and I weren't able to sustain our marriage and we separated, I became even more convinced that my job was to make sure I remained available to my two daughters. Developing a strong, unbreakable bond with them became one of the most important things in the world to me.

But it wasn't easy, primarily because I had nothing to emulate. Many men move into the role of father quite easily, smoothly, because their own fathers had always been there as examples. They could either duplicate their fathers' strength or eliminate their weaknesses. But I had none of that. All I had was absence, emptiness. I didn't know the elements that made fathers successful or the things to avoid. So I would find myself watching fathers, trying to figure out what worked or didn't work and how to incorporate it into my own fathering style.

My goal was to break the generational cycle of dysfunction that hung over my family. I already had a failed marriage; I didn't want a failed fatherhood, too. But I had to be honest with myself and acknowledge that I needed help, that I had many shortcomings in this area. I knew my goal would be impossible to reach if I didn't figure out how to fix them.

The world is not a perfect place; none of our families are perfect, either. All of us who come out of "broken" or dysfunctional homes first must comfort ourselves with the knowledge that we're not responsible for our family situations. I had to bear some of the shame, the embarrassment, and the lack of security from what my father did, but none of it was my fault. So while embarrassment might be an understandable response, I could not burden myself with guilt. Just as some people inherit wealth, I inherited dysfunction. And just as those who inherit wealth should not act as if the wealth accrues some sort of merit on them, granting them a superiority over those whose beginnings were more humble, you shouldn't be humiliated if you're on the other side of the ledger, grappling with family dysfunction, because you had nothing to do with it.

Those of us who come from dysfunction must take an important step toward healing. We have to admit that we are scarred and understand where our scars are located. I realized perhaps the most damaging consequence of my father's abandonment was a feeling I retained, deep in my psyche, that I was unworthy, that I had been rejected. When you grow up believing that you have been rejected by the man whose genes helped to form you, whose name is stamped on you, whose face is clearly visible in yours, you can't help but embark on a dire search for validation. That's what I got from James Brown and Jesse Jackson and Rev. Bill Jones, a widely respected religious leader in Brooklyn—more than seeing them as father figures to emulate, I saw them as important men who could validate me. By spending time with me when my father wouldn't, by advising me when my father had not a word of advice to offer, they gave me a sense of self-worth that I didn't even realize I had lost until I got it from them. My thinking was, if these talented and influential men were taking time with me, then I must not be some worthless kid from the hood who had no value and nothing to offer.

When you come from a childhood as shattering as mine was, you have to be honest about your insecurities and your burning questions. Whatever process you come up with to deal with these issues, whether it's prayer or meditation or a therapist's couch, you must step into that den of painful self-inquiry and find some answers for yourself. If you don't, the insecurities and the questions will remain buried deep in your psyche and become a threat to everything you do—lurking, biding their time, ready to spring forth at the most inopportune moments and sink you with self-doubt and self-sabotage. If you come from dysfunction and you don't grapple with it, bearing the inevitable pain, it can become a permanent fixture in your personality.

I was in my twenties when James Brown took me with him to the White House, and on that day, he told me that he wanted me to style my hair like his. For me, it wasn't about the hairstyle; it was the satisfaction of having this man asking me to emulate him, something that had never happened with my own father. That's why I didn't even give it a second thought—he could have been telling me that from then on, we were going to wear short pants. I still would have done it. Of course, on the surface, it looked as if I was just copying my idol, but the deeper point was that he was giving me the validation I so desperately needed. Had I known beforehand that I was going through these psychological trials, that I badly wanted validation, I might have responded differently to the hairstyle.

Now that I have the benefit of hindsight, I see how the traumas of my early years continued to reach far into my adult years and affect my experiences as a parent. Although I grew up swirling around in a stew of need and dysfunction, I think I was able to break the cycle and give my daughters a stable foundation to launch them into adulthood. Whenever I could, I would bring them with me, whether it was to the White House or just to a chicken dinner at some local event. Even now, although they are grown, I have a long-standing dinner date with them every week.

Certainly, their childhoods were out of the ordinary, because their father's job was the farthest thing from a nine-to-five imaginable, always on the road, always fighting a new cause. But they could always be sure of one thing: Their father was nearby, anxious to shower them with all the love I could manage.

4

LEARNING FROM FLAWED LEADERS

O ur leaders aren't always going to be perfect, but we can still learn a great deal from them about how to live our lives. This message was delivered to me with force and clarity by the great Adam Clayton Powell Jr.

As I moved into adolescence, I became fascinated with Powell, whose father had been pastor of Harlem's iconic Abyssinian Baptist Church from 1908 to 1936. Adam Jr. was a huge figure in Harlem during his civil rights activist days, using rent strikes and public campaigns to force businesses to treat blacks fairly. He utilized the picket line to force the World's Fair to hire more blacks in 1939. Two years later, he led a bus boycott to force the Transit Authority to hire more black workers. After succeeding his father as pastor of Abyssinian, Adam was elected to the New York City Council in 1941, the first black council member in New York history. He was elected to the U.S. House of Representatives in 1944, the first black congressman in New York State history. Once he got to Congress, Powell immediately became its racial conscience, as he was eager to take on the racists and segregationists who had been roaming the congressional floor for decades. Adam wasn't afraid of anybody. His courage, brilliance, and outspokenness made him a figure of immense pride in the black community.

I would go up to see him at Abyssinian on Sundays, entranced by his electrifying sermons. I would hang out after church and find a way to attach myself to his entourage. This was the kind of preacher I wanted to be. Powell knew my pastor, Bishop Washington, so he let me hang around him. He had a man on his staff named Odell Clark and a driver named Jack Packard, and even though I was just twelve, they would call me and tell me when he was coming to town. They got used to me being around, and Adam was intrigued by me, this kid preacher following him around like a puppy. I think my fascination with him probably flattered him. He had begun his political decline and was accused of misusing public funds, eventually being stripped of his chairmanship of the House's powerful Labor and Education Committee, a position that he had wielded like a talisman in helping President Lyndon Johnson enact pivotal legislation in his War on Poverty.

Congress had voted to prevent Adam from taking his seat until the House Judiciary Committee completed an investigation, even though he had been reelected by his constituents. The Supreme Court eventually ruled that

Congress had acted unconstitutionally in keeping Powell from taking a seat to which he had been elected.

In the midst of his troubles, Adam appeared on the *David Frost Show*, a popular evening talk show at the time. Frost asked Powell how he would describe himself, since he had been a member of Congress for more than twenty years, had been the pastor of the largest Baptist denominational church, had been married three times, and had an untold number of mistresses.

Adam leaned back, puffed on his cigar, and said, "Adam Powell doesn't give a damn."

At first, Frost didn't appear to understand. "What do you mean?" he asked.

So Adam repeated it. "I don't give a damn," he said. "I don't care what anybody thinks. As long as it's not illegal, immoral, or fattening, I'm going to live my life."

I was amazed, exhilarated. Can you imagine the impact of that kind of bravado on an impressionable fourteen-year-old boy? I yearned to get to the point where I could be so bold and uncaring about what people thought. And when I was early in my career, during the Bernard Goetz, Howard Beach, and Tawana Brawley years, that's exactly how I was. My mind-set was, *I'm going to do me, I'm gonna be me, I don't care what anybody thinks.*

But one day, as I started to mature, I realized that Adam's mind-set was flawed. That was not leadership reflected in that way of thinking; it was selfishness. When you have accepted the mantle of leadership, when you want to ascend to the level where people can comfortably call you a leader, you must accept the reality that people have the right to expect you to be different, better, more evolved than everybody else. If they are going to invest their faith and their hopes and their ambitions in you, then they have the right to expect that you are going to be the kind of leader who does care what people think. With all due respect to one of my early idols, they have the right to expect you to give a damn.

I've seen this over and over. When you go too far in not giving a damn, then you become the caricature rather than the conduit. So if I'm oppressed and I need you to be the one to bring my message, I don't need for you to be distracted by whom you're going to bed with, being intoxicated in public, not giving a damn. Because all of that quickly gets in the way of the work at hand.

After going through the Adam period, with the memory of that David Frost interview stamped in my mind, I eventually saw a transformation in my thinking. I started to realize that you need to give a damn, not because of your adversaries but because of whom you claim you want to serve. This was an extremely important revelation for me. If you're going to call yourself a leader, do you love the people you want to lead enough to discipline yourself? If you don't, then are you worthy of leading them? It goes back to the Bible, Luke 12: "To whom much is given much is required."

Let's bring this idea down to a more personal level, to those of us who are trying to be leaders of our families. If you're a father, do you love your wife and children and family life enough to summon the discipline to turn away from the pretty girl in accounting with the come-hither smile? Is half an hour with her in a stairwell or a hotel somewhere spectacular enough for you to throw away all that happiness and possibly wreck your children in the process? If you're a mom, are you going to succumb to the nice guy in marketing who listens patiently to all your complaints about being bored or unsatisfied in your marriage, one day finding yourself in his arms and in his bed, or are you going to be strong enough for the sake of your family to walk up to your husband and ask him to help you fix what's broken? If you're a business owner tempted to cut corners or do something illicit to bring in more cash for your family, think about what might happen to that family if you were hauled away to jail. Being a leader is hard, whether you're leading a nation, a community, a company, or a family. You're going to need vast reserves of discipline, patience—and love.

In all of the work I've done over the years, I've always been motivated much more by the people I aim to serve than by any accolades or pats on the back from the media or the politically powerful. It's an inclination that I believe can be traced back to my earliest influences, being drawn to men like Powell not because of the power he had accrued but because of the changes he was able to make in the lives of those he led.

5

YOU NEED TO KNOW
WHEN TO QUIT IT

Two great men from very different spheres of influence taught me a crucial lesson about the importance of timing: knowing when to move on.

Even before the end is nigh, as Adam Clayton Powell Jr. showed me, you have to start thinking about it, working on an exit plan. If you don't, if you blithely pass the days thinking you're going to stick around forever, you end up leading yourself into ruination.

Powell was dying of cancer and had just narrowly lost in the Democratic primary to Charlie Rangel. The year was 1971, and for the previous two decades, Adam had been the king of Harlem. Everybody wanted him to come back fighting, to take Harlem back from this young upstart Rangel, who had been in the state assembly for four years. I traveled up to Harlem from Brooklyn that Sunday after the election to see him at

Abyssinian. He had announced that he was resigning from the church and wasn't going to fight Rangel. He was gone, retired, and heading to Bimini, the island in the Bahamas where he had a home and spent a lot of his time.

When I found out that he planned to leave, I asked Odell Clark, his assistant, "Are you kidding me? Why is he gonna do that?"

Clark said, "You go talk to him, kid." Powell and his people all used to call me "kid."

There was a long hall at Abyssinian that you had to walk down to get to the steps on the side of the church that led to the street. I ran around to the side and saw him in the hall, already coming out of his office. He was holding hands with Darlene Expose, his girlfriend at the time, as he walked down the stairs.

"Reverend Powell!" I said.

He turned around and saw me. "Hey, kid," he said, and he patted me on the head.

"You can't leave us," I said. "You've got to run. We've gotta get the seat back from Charlie Rangel! What are we going to do?"

He looked at me closely. He said, "Kid, one day, you're gonna grow up and be a great man. Always remember this: Know when to hit it, and know when to quit it." He paused. "For me, it's quitting time."

But I didn't want to hear that. "Well, what are we gonna do?"

"I'm going fishing," he said. "I don't know what y'all are gonna do."

He patted me on the head again. Then they were gone. It was the last time I ever saw him alive.

Despite it all, he went out a legend, because he didn't disgrace himself by trying to hold on too long. I'll always remember what he said: *Know when to quit it*. When quitting time comes for me, I'm gone.

I think a lot of my colleagues in public office get into trouble because they lose sight of the point, the reason that drove them into the career in the first place. You've got to consciously decide early on, when you get your shot, what are you going to do with it? You've got to come ready for execution. You have to aspire to leadership for a reason, not just because it's your season, not because you think it's your time to lead. You must have specific things you want to achieve, benchmarks that drive you. Otherwise, if it's just about the position and the power, you won't ever want to let it go. But if you had goals, once you have crossed them all off your list, then you can walk away from the job with a smile and a great deal of satisfaction. I can name many leaders who got seduced by the position and lost sight of the goals.

When I meet young people who tell me they aspire to leadership, my first question is, "To what end?" If they can't answer that question, then I have to conclude that they don't really deserve leadership; they're just trying to be celebrities. We have got enough celebrities. We need some leaders.

The lack of mentorship is a serious problem in the political realm, across parties and ideologies and racial backgrounds. We all need to be more intentional about bringing along the next generation. All of us, when we have achieved at a certain level, should be asked, "Who are your mentees? Who are you bringing along?" Young people aren't doing enough to seek out mentors, and older leaders aren't doing enough to reach back. It is a particularly acute problem in the black community, where you often have a talented young newcomer taking on the old, established lion, who is so eager to hold on to his seat that he will stoop to embarrassing levels to discredit the newcomer. We see this all the time. I think that when you have been denied power and influence for so long, those who break through and gain some power are going to be desperate to keep it. That's just human nature. But there's a difference between natural competitiveness and trying unduly to maintain something you should no longer be trying to maintain. I don't care who you are, at some point, your skills wane, your luster wears off. You should want to go out as a respected figure, rather than playing dirty and undoing all of the goodwill you accumulated. Granted, this is a lot easier said than done. But I think you know when you've lost it, whether you are an orator, an athlete, or a leader. When you don't recognize the signs, the consequences can be dire.

Muhammad Ali told me that at the end of his career, in the ring, he could see the opening against his opponent, but he couldn't move his fist fast enough to get there. That's the sign it's time to bow out, although too many fighters are not willing to act on it. But if you don't act, you might wind up on your back, your legacy forever tarnished. It's so enticing to try to hold on, to give it one more shot. But what you've got to think about is how hard it was for you to get there. Do you really want to undermine all that work, all those years of blood and sweat you poured into making your name mean something? I saw guys wind up on their backs, and I don't want to be that guy. But if you see me slipping, losing my ability to get to that opening, like Ali, then do me a favor—slide me a note to let me know that it might be time to quit it. But please, be kind.

6

NEVER REST ON YOUR LAURELS

No matter how high you soar, how many accolades you collect, maybe the most important lesson to hold close can be summarized with few words: Don't rest on your laurels.

I came to see the importance of this lesson by closely watching Dr. William Jones. When I was twelve years old, my pastor, Bishop Washington, knowing of my interest in social justice, introduced me to Dr. Jones, who was a lion in the black New York religious community. Dr. Jones was a deep thinker with a fire in his belly for social justice and a hunger to help the poor and oppressed. He was head of the 5,000-member Bethany Baptist Church in Bedford-Stuyvesant, the son and the grandson of Baptist preachers, an academic theologian with degrees from the University of Kentucky and Crozer Theological Seminary, the same institution that helped mold Dr. King. As the New York chairman of Operation Breadbasket, the economic development arm of the Southern Christian Leadership Conference (SCLC), Dr. Jones was the kind of preacher I aspired to be. In Reverend Jones I found a psychic fit, a leader who wanted to get out there and confront authority on behalf of his people.

Reverend Jones died the same year as James Brown, in 2006, removing two great influences from my life in rapid succession. But Reverend Jones told me something a year before he passed that will always stay with me.

He said, "Alfred, I only fear three things."

"What's that?" I asked.

"I fear God, I fear living past my mourners, and I fear drowning in shallow waters," he said, his booming voice filling his office.

He saw the quizzical look on my face and kept going.

"I don't want to be so old that when I die, there's nobody around who knew my glory. I still want to be relevant when I die. And I don't want to have scaled the oceans, beaten the whales, outrun the sharks, and then come into the shallow water around the kids playing in the sandbar and drown in the shallow waters."

He turned to me with a look that was almost haunting. "You're on your way now; you will make your mark in history," he said. "But watch out for the shallow water. Don't go out on some shallow foolishness."

Examples abound in popular culture of leaders brought down by indiscretions, usually connected to sex or money—from Rev. Jimmy Swaggart to South Carolina Gov. Mark Sanford, from Detroit Mayor Kwame Kilpatrick to Rep. Anthony Weiner. Leaders who soiled years of accomplishment with carelessness, recklessness, and extremely poor judgment.

It's a powerful lesson, because once you ascend to a certain level, the temptation is always there to relax, to get sloppy. You're thinking, *Oh, boy, I can have fun now*. And then you find yourself gasping for air in that shallow water. Next thing you know, you've undone decades of hard work.

If you ever find yourself flailing about in shallow water, you must remember the first step to saving yourself and getting back on track: Stand up.

7

BE AUTHENTIC

I am powerfully reminded of the need to be authentic, to be *real*, every time I go out into the community to preach or meet my people at some event. When I am invited to give a sermon or to speak at a church anniversary or an awards dinner, I make sure I come down from the pulpit and spend as much time as possible mixing and socializing with people, taking pictures, shaking hands, accepting hugs and kisses. I might have a million people watching me every night on television and a half-million people listening to me every day on the radio, but it's the regular folks at the church events and in the community who sustain me and make me what I am, not the TV show on MSNBC. It's those grandmas on fixed incomes who scrape their quarters together to make it down to the church to hear me. When there is no more MSNBC show, those women will still be there for me. I'm more concerned with them saying, "I'm with you, Reverend Al, I'm praying for you, don't let us down," than I am concerned about some editorial in the newspaper or on a website slamming me.

Now, I understand that there are others in leadership, even in the black community, who have to deal with the editorial writer in the cubicle, because they have to run for office. I get that; that's their lane. But my lane is over here, fighting for the grandma in Ohio, the black kid in the hood who can't find a job, the family whose child has just been victimized by the police or by a fake neighborhood watchman because of how he looked. Those are the people Reverend Jones always put at the top of his list. I have always tried to do the same, following the lead of my pastor. As long as I keep my focus on them, then I know I'll be all right. Once you lose your touch with the people you're supposed to be serving, sooner or later, you become irrelevant.

I recently spoke at a church in the Midwest, and just before I left, someone asked me if I could go back up on the stage and take pictures with a bunch of kids who were there. I didn't hesitate. It was so easy for me to remember when I was one of those kids. It was me standing there taking a picture with Adam Powell. It was me standing there taking a picture with Jesse Jackson. And I know there may come a day when one of those kids will think, *I don't have to be an athlete, I can be a leader, like Al Sharpton.*

Even during my sermon that night, I glanced up to the balcony and saw a group of kids from the church. There were about fifteen or twenty of them, mostly fidgeting in their seats and trying to make it through my sermon. But if you looked closely, you could notice that two of them weren't fidgeting at all. They were engrossed, taking in every word. That was me fifty years ago, sitting in Washington Temple, studying every utterance and nuance of every preacher who came through there.

You never know whom you may touch, so you have to make yourself available to that, open yourself up to the possibility that staying a little longer after the speech, wading into the crowd to shake hands and take pictures, answering every question that is asked of you, might be the crucial moment when something clicks in a young mind, when a seed is planted, and that kid blossoms into a great leader. These great leaders always made themselves available to me, so it's only right for me to do the same. I was this chubby little kid from the hood. Why would I turn out to be anything? Why would a great leader think it was important to have a word with me? But they did. Those young people, that grandma on a fixed income, it is their plight that I'm trying to bear. They are the ones I serve.

I think some of the most disappointing moments of my career have come when I met leaders who were leading people they didn't even like. Forget love—they see their flock as just props, extras to help them reach their life goals, backdrops in their photo ops. I think when you have those feelings about your constituents, they can feel it. You can only fake the affection for so long. People know. James Brown used to tell me that people can feel you before they can hear you. Especially people who have been oppressed. They have been exploited so much that their antennas are always up, checking for authenticity, kicking the tires, making sure you are real.

They know who's authentic and who's not. They can't even tell you how they know, can't even describe what is missing. They just know.

So that's why it's so important for leaders to be themselves. Even if sometimes that means not being the perfect candidate, or the perfect pastor, or the perfect principal. People will accept you and your mistakes much more readily if they feel you're being real. What they won't accept is a phony. I've made a ton of mistakes in my career, but the people I was trying to lead didn't hold them against me, because they could see the content of my heart. They could feel it. It's like the saying I hear all the time in politics: It's not the crime, it's the cover-up. You make the mistake, people understand. But when you try to disguise it and play them for the fool, that's when you're going to pay dearly.

The Bible is filled with examples of the importance of authenticity and the many rewards that will flow to you when you don't try to be something that you're not. When Moses found out that he was actually an Israelite and not an Egyptian, he went and found his people and became a great leader to them, rather than trying to live more comfortably as one of the ruling Egyptians.

When God called Gideon to lead the Israelites from oppression, Gideon didn't try to hide his fear and pretend he was some heroic figure. No, he asked God to prove Himself before Gideon would commit to taking on a massive army. So that's when God drenched the fleece in dew, to demonstrate His power.

I think it's only natural to wrestle with yourself when you are faced with the opportunity to be something you're not. Who among us doesn't want to be perceived as smarter or braver or grander than we really are? But it is when you win that wrestling match with yourself that you begin to approach greatness.

Those who listen to me on the pulpit or in front of the mic might notice that I mix a lot of humor into my orations. It was always a part of my personality to be funny, but at an early age, I decided to develop and use humor in my sermonizing. I think it's extremely important when converting people to make them comfortable; it adds a great deal to your authenticity. You have to let people know that you are not dropped out of heaven onto earth like some flawless gift of God. That's not going to get you as far as letting them see that you came through the same insecurities, the same anxieties, the same fears, the same temptations that they did. I came from the ground up; I didn't come from the sky down. When people realize that about you, they can relate to you better and therefore are more open to your message.

For instance, when I talk about women, I'm honest about the changes I went through after my marriage ended, when I was trying to date a lot of younger women, stumbling through the stereotypical middle-age crisis, trying to prove I was still young and vital. But one day, I woke up and thought, *You can go out with a twenty-year-old girl, but you're certainly not twenty anymore. You're not fooling anybody but yourself.* That is an entirely different message from me preaching about it from a lofty perch, as if I'm up on Mount Sinai. Similarly, I can talk in a personal way about vanity because I went through it myself, when my vanity outran my sanity, that period of wanting to be in the newspaper, rather than being more concerned about what I'm saying and whether I'm using it for good. That's real. And the more real you are about your own shortcomings, the easier it is for you to help somebody get past his or hers. If you can't be real about your own shortcomings, then you haven't gotten over them. I can't concede and confess openly to foolish pride or worthless vanity or middle-age insecurity if I'm still wracked by them.

In the ministry and in the civil rights movement, I've seen many men try to model themselves after a great leader who came before them, only to falter because of their inauthenticity. Rather than find their own voice and style, they mimic great pastors such as Gardner Taylor, C. L. Franklin, or Billy Graham. But as a firm believer in God and the idea that He gives everyone his or her own purpose, I don't think He gives duplicate callings. I don't believe He calls Joe and then has Joe 1, Joe 2, and Joe 3. No, that calling was for Joe. You can learn from Joe. But He doesn't want you to be a duplicate blessing of Joe. You have your own blessing—you just have to clear your head and go find it. Yes, as I grew, I studied many other ministers, closely scrutinizing every minute detail of their style. But when it came time for me to step into the pulpit, I tried to do my own thing, knowing God had something special for Sharpton. Mine was not an overflow of theirs; I had my own flow.

What's the danger in the duplicate? Well, no matter how talented you are as a mimic, it's never going to be the real thing. A copy is never as good as the original.

There is also the question of authenticity. People can sense the fakeness. If they're watching a copy, somewhere in their subconscious, they're going to wonder, is the copy a true believer, or has he just perfected somebody else's act? You can't convince people that they should believe in you and follow you if they don't think you believe it yourself. They won't feel totally comfortable with you. They won't trust you. Eventually, they will turn their backs on you. That's one of the reasons I make sure I'm always working in the community, meeting with local leaders, speaking at churches across America, so I can stay connected to people. Speaking to the public through a television screen or a radio signal holds no comparison to standing in the pulpit and looking into their faces, seeing the anxiety and the fear and the hope all mixed together in their eyes as they listen to you, hoping that your words will bring them some sort of relief, even if just for the night. No matter what I am doing, I can never give up that authentic connection with people. It is an essential part of who I am.

8

DON'T BE AFRAID TO CHANGE
AND EVOLVE

Just like the rest of America, I have seen an enormous trans-formation over the years in my views on homosexuality and gay rights. I believe passionately in the equal rights of gays, and I have spoken out forcefully on issues such as same-sex marriage for more than a decade. But if I am being honest, I must admit that I didn't start in a place of enlightenment.

I grew up in the streets of Brooklyn, running around with kids who weren't exactly progressive on this issue. I remember freely using the word *faggot* to describe a guy who was not aggressive. It was just something that we did, letting that word easily fall from our lips without really thinking about the deeper meaning. We just knew that to be gay was to be soft, and to be soft was the most devastating label that a black boy in the hood could endure. When I look back on those years, my first thought—perhaps *rationalization* is the right word here—

is that we weren't being homophobic in our use of that word. It was just a word that had entered the young black male lexicon, just like a long list of other profanities that I won't mention here. We didn't necessarily connect it to an actual person who was a homosexual.

Or so I used to think.

But as I have reflected more on this question over the years, I have to concede that those early rationalizations weren't necessarily true. It is a homophobic term, a word directly and unmistakably connected to a general revulsion against the choices and lifestyle of gays. There's no escaping that. You can't try to sever a nasty word from its roots and pretend it no longer has any sting because you have declared it so.

After all, I would take great offense if somebody called me *nigger*, even if they professed to be free of any racial prejudice. If the member of the targeted group finds offense in the word, then the word is offensive. You don't get to use it and also to conclude that no one can take offense because you didn't mean any offense. Words have history, an etymology that can't be avoided.

The idea of homosexuality wasn't an abstraction to me. I wasn't some naive child who grew up without knowing any gays. No, in fact, they were all around me. Anyone who has ever spent time in a black church knows exactly what I'm talking about. The black church has a long history of employing openly gay men in prominent positions, particularly connected to the choirs and the music. While this might appear to veer into the realm of stereotype, it's hard to escape this reality if you've been in as many black churches as I have.

I also had gays in my family, one cousin in particular who wasn't about to let me keep the issue at arm's length. No, from a fairly young age, she would challenge me.

"Why do you get to choose who I love and who loves me?" she asked me one day.

I was a child of the church, so I had my answer ready. "Well, it's a sin. It's what we believe in the church."

But this woman was always persistent. "But as you got older, you decided which things were just church dogma and what was biblical—so now you're going to decide for me?"

That definitely broadened my perspective, made me start considering the issue from another angle. And with her words driving me, I started to fit the issue into my broader outlook on justice and equality and soon came to realize something important about civil rights activism: It cannot be applied discriminately. If you see yourself as an enemy of injustice, then you must be an enemy of all injustice. You can't just pick and choose which injustices you're going to fight. That's the height of hypocrisy. And it's also shortsighted—and dangerous.

When I was a teenager, I was appointed youth director of the New York branch of Operation Breadbasket, the group started by SCLC and Dr. Martin Luther King to improve the economic conditions of the black community through the use of boycotts and economic pressure. Not too long after, I decided to start my own organization, which I called the National Youth Movement.

I needed advice to get my group off the ground, so the first person I went to see was Bayard Rustin. Rustin was a brilliant leader and a gifted organizer who had been a guiding force behind the establishment of the SCLC and an influential adviser to Dr. King, whose leadership skills Rustin recognized early on. Rustin was widely known as the architect behind the pivotal 1963 March on Washington. He was the Socrates of the movement. But from the standpoint of leaders in the civil rights movement, Rustin had one big problem: He was gay. He had even been arrested in 1953 for engaging in a homosexual act, which was against the law in many parts of the country. Because he was viewed by many inside the movement as a pariah, Rustin had to lead from the shadows, allowing other men to be the public face of the movement while he had to be content to stay in the background. A. Philip Randolph got the credit for leading the March on Washington, but Rustin did much of the crucial planning.

Rustin had an office on Park Avenue South in Manhattan, in the headquarters of the United Federation of Teachers, the city teachers union. When I walked into his office, I was overwhelmed by all of the African masks, sculptures, and art I saw everywhere. It was like walking from a staid Midtown office into a museum. I had never seen that much African art in one place in my life. Although Rustin was from Pennsylvania, he spoke with a British accent.

"Explain to me your program, young man," he said. "What are you planning to do?"

I told him I wanted to work on voter registration, even though I was too young to vote. I discussed wanting to fight for community control of education in New York. This was during the battle in Brooklyn over community control of the schools. Rustin was supporting the teachers over the local community in the fight, so we debated that a bit. I asked him to speak at the opening luncheon my organization was having at the New York Hilton.

"I will speak at your luncheon," he said. "Who else are you having?"

Congresswoman Shirley Chisholm, who was running for president, was also going to speak, and I told him that I was the youth director of her campaign.

"Well, I'm not supporting Shirley," he said, "but I'll come. And I'm going to give you five hundred dollars. Do you have any money you need to start?"

Believe it or not, I hadn't even thought about money.

"I guess I do need money," I said.

So he handed me a check for $500 to start my organization, the first contribution I got. He followed through and spoke at the luncheon. We actually stayed in touch through the years until he died in 1987.

I have an enormous problem with the way the black community downplayed the contributions of men like Bayard Rustin to the cause of black liberation because of our homophobia. If we're really serious about honoring the importance of black history, how are we going to write Rustin out of the history books because of his sexual orientation, pretend that he wasn't a crucial figure in our fight for freedom in this country because he was attracted to men? This just does not sit well with me. It's tragically wrong.

Likewise, are we going to pretend that James Baldwin, because he was openly gay, wasn't one of the giants not only of black literary history but of American literary history? We're supposed to discount his forceful and courageous voice, his perceptive and scathing critiques of American society, his unique and groundbreaking talent, because his lifestyle didn't conform to the tastes of the majority? If you're a black nationalist, firmly committed to the advancement of black people here and around the world, you're not going to put Baldwin near the top of the list of iconic figures in black history because you don't like gays?

You can't write Bayard Rustin out of civil rights history. You can't write James Baldwin out of literary history. We don't have a problem honoring black leaders who have been adulterous, who have been involved in financial scandals, who were some of the most narcissistic, unpleasant individuals you could ever come across. You could sleep with half of your congregation and still be a revered pastor—as long as those congregants were women.

I have been fighting since I was fourteen years old to push our society to recognize the value of every human life, struggling to force the state to acknowledge the importance of human dignity, so how can I sit by and think that this treatment of gays is OK?

How can I call myself a civil rights leader if I am blind to this grossly unjust civil right being trampled right in front of my face?

Indeed, as a nation that sees each of its denizens imbued with the right to life, liberty, and the pursuit of happiness, how can we accept the denial of this right to such a significant portion of the American populace?

Is there anything more un-American than that?

I would like for my country to view gay rights as one of the great human rights issues of our time.

My evolution on this issue has also demonstrated to me the importance of staying strong and resolute in your beliefs, even if you're confronted with denunciation and attack.

I came out in support of gay marriage in 2003, long before President Obama made it a major issue in the black community. This was as I prepared to run for president myself in 2004, and I think it took a lot of people by surprise. Those who knew me and were familiar with my thinking had watched me evolve over the years on the issue. But for others, having a Baptist preacher publicly announce support for gay marriage was certainly unexpected, and it was a big deal.

Although my announcement might have created some buzz in gay circles, it certainly wasn't of much political benefit to me. I wasn't running for the gay vote; I had much more to lose in my own base, which was African-Americans, than I had to gain by picking up political support from gays. It was the same calculation for President Obama, which made the accusations kind of ridiculous that he did it for political gain. Even in the civil rights community, I was standing out there nearly alone when I made my announcement. Andrew Young, the iconic civil rights leader, Atlanta mayor, and former U.S. ambassador to the United Nations, was one of the few who publicly stood with me on the issue.

After the announcement, I had prominent ministers, men I've known for decades, tell me that they wouldn't let me preach in their churches if I was going to stand up at the pulpit and take that position. A pastor of a prominent church where I went every year to preach the anniversary program called me after my announcement.

"Doc, I don't think I can have you this year," he said.

"I understand," I said.

"Can't you moderate your views a little bit?"

"What do you mean?" I asked him. I wanted to hear him say it.

"Why don't you just say you're with civil unions, not marriage?" he said.

"Why?"

"It's just not moral," he answered.

"Moral? So let me get this straight, Reverend. I should say gays can shack up, but they can't marry? That sounds moral to you? I thought we preached against shacking up, Reverend."

Years later, after I got the MSNBC show, I got another call from this reverend, asking if I could come back and preach the anniversary program again.

"Can you come back, Doc?" he asked.

"I'd love to," I said. But I couldn't let him off that easy. "I want to preach about Steve and Ray getting married."

He started laughing. I did wind up preaching his anniversary program that year, and I refrained from preaching about Steve and Ray. But I found the transformation amusing, reminding me of the old expression: Success is the greatest deodorant. When you get successful, all your stench is gone.

The hypocrisy of the black church on this issue is absolutely breathtaking to me. As I said before, anyone who has spent more than five minutes in a typical black church knows how huge a presence gays are, particularly in the music ministry. But I've never seen a minister get up in the pulpit and say, "I'm not accepting gay tithes. I'm not accepting the offering from any gays." If you really believe it's sinful, go back through your church records, and for the church members you know are gay, refund all the money they've contributed to the church over the years. If you really think it's a sin, shut down the choir, and ban anyone who is gay from participating.

Clearly, that's never going to happen. So what these ministers are saying is that they will accommodate gays as long as it's in their best interest to accept them. *Let's just not talk about it. Don't ask, don't tell. I'll continue to take your tithes and offerings, let you run my choir, but I don't think you have the right to be you. And I won't marry you. I won't acknowledge who you are. I won't even allow you to be married outside the church—and I will denounce those who decide that they will allow it.*

But just keep those tithes coming.

To me, that's the height of hypocrisy.

The history of black thought on homosexuality roughly follows the same evolutionary arc in this country as that of the mainstream community, and as a group, blacks are among the most religious in the United States. So you take this passionate religious conviction and combine it with the black church's long-standing opposition to homosexuality, and you will get a community still grappling with gay rights—and in many cases, standing staunchly opposed to it.

I often hear African-Americans expressing contempt at the fact that gays have begun to co-opt the language and methods of the civil rights movement. As the argument goes, the fight for equal rights for gays can never be compared to the fight for equal rights for African-Americans, because gays can conceal their sexual identity and assimilate anytime they want, while blacks never have that option. But the issue is rights, not levels or degrees of discrimination or victimization. Because the victimization of African-Americans was harsher or more widespread or more easily enforced, gays are therefore not entitled to the same rights as African-Americans? Is that what we're saying here? Why are we setting a minimum standard for discrimination that another group has to reach before we can accede that they shouldn't be discriminated against? Shouldn't the goal be for all of us to be free? If we have 90 percent experiencing discrimination, and they only have 10 percent, then they aren't entitled to equal protection? (And last time I checked, black people are allowed to get married.)

Along with the criticism I have heard on same-sex marriage is the idea that someone like me isn't supposed to speak out on behalf of gays. I'm supposed to stay in my lane, fight injustices against black folks, and not get distracted by the battles of nonblacks. But anyone who tries to put me in that box doesn't understand who I am. You can't try to limit a freedom fighter from standing for people's freedoms. This is an attack that we've heard leveled against black leaders for years—from Malcolm X and the Black Panthers to Dr. King and Rev. Jesse Jackson. *Why are you worrying yourself about the Vietnam War, or poor white people, or undocumented immigrants? That's somebody else's struggle.* But you can't take care of black folks in isolation. We are a global community, connected to the larger world. And you can't help your own community without making alliances with like-minded people in other communities. That was my thinking when I decided to take a public stand with Puerto Ricans against the U.S. Navy in Vieques. Black people can't just go off to a corner somewhere and fight for our space in a vacuum. It doesn't make practical sense. And if you're committed to what's good and right, you're committed to it across the board. You don't segregate your passion for liberation and freedom based on the melanin count of the victims. That's totally antithetical to the whole idea of being a freedom fighter.

When it comes to the nation's struggles with gay marriage, let us take a step back and consider how this looks to outsiders, perhaps someone from one of those Muslim countries that Americans are constantly condemning because of their willingness to rule the land by the laws of their religion. We are quick to berate countries in the Middle East and Africa that are intent on imposing Sharia law, lecturing them about how undemocratic they are, about how they should consider separating church and state the way we do. We even invaded Iraq and used the spread of democracy as one of our justifications—this after the "weapons of mass destruction" argument failed to stand up to the facts. We Americans are so infatuated with our democracy that we believe we can sprinkle it across the globe like topsoil and just watch it grow, naively believing it'll take root in countries that have been invested in other governing systems for centuries. But as we scold Pakistan and Syria for their religious fundamentalism and preach to them about the healing powers of democracy, if we turned our gaze back on ourselves, we would quickly see how hypocritical we must look to the outside world.

When we try to deny rights to same-sex couples based on our religious principles, how are we not acting out our own form of religious fundamentalism? We look down upon these other countries for requiring women to wear veils, but I can remember when I was growing up in the Church of God in Christ, it was considered a sin for women to wear pants and lipstick. When we went to a gospel competition and I saw a first lady of one of the big churches wearing pants, I scurried over to my mother and said, "Ma, look, she's going to hell because she has on pants!"

But the church changed, evolved, and was overtaken by a measure of modernity. We need to keep this in mind when we get so set in our positions, so rigidly opposed to change. I'm as firmly ensconced in the principles of the black church as anyone; I started preaching when I was just four years old! If I can evolve in my own thinking on gay marriage, I am convinced that we can all do it. In fact, we must, for the sake of our children and our grandchildren. The last thing we want is for future generations to look back on our politics and shake their heads at the rampant bigotry that masqueraded as conventional wisdom—much the same way that we shake our heads now at the segregationists who ruled the South fifty years ago. What was once unthinkable is now commonplace.

I want to know that when a child in 2063 looks back to study American society at the turn of the last century and she comes across the name Al Sharpton, she will see that I stood proudly for justice and equality—for every member of our society.

9

VALUE FAMILY, VALUE COMMUNITY, AND, MOST IMPORTANT, VALUE YOURSELF

With the publication in 1965 of the U.S. Labor Department report "The Negro Family: The Case for National Action," Daniel Patrick Moynihan shaped an entire generation of analysis about the plight of African-Americans. An assistant secretary of labor at the time, Moynihan, who would soon become a U.S. senator from New York, wrote a persuasive treatise that not only deeply influenced President Lyndon Johnson in his crafting of the War on Poverty but also established the direction and tenor of the national conversation about the black community for years to come.

Moynihan's conclusion, largely derived from statistics, was presented right at the top of his report: "At the heart of the deterioration of the fabric of Negro society is the deterioration of the Negro family. It is the fundamental source of the weakness of the Negro community at the present time."

This was the overarching thesis of his report, which presented graphs, charts, and pages of powerful testimony to prove its insight. But right from the start, I think Moynihan got it all wrong, and much of the debate about black pathology over the past nearly fifty years has suffered as a result.

By using the white family and white society as his point of comparison, Moynihan essentially missed the fundamental truth of black American life: Black success has always derived from community, not from family.

In Moynihan's paper and in much of the societal discussion since then, there has been a hazy nostalgia for a return to solid nuclear families, to strong patriarchal units, to *Leave It to Beaver* family unity and family values. *If we could only get back to that time, black pathology will disappear*, the thinking goes.

Well, my response to all of this nostalgia is, back to when?

I've never known a time when we didn't have serious issues in the black family. As Moynihan pointed out correctly, much of it emanated from our history, a history during which it was against the law for blacks even to have a family. My great-grandfather, as the *New York Daily News* discovered in 2007, was the property of the late Sen. Strom Thurmond's family in Edgefield County, South Carolina. That's just two generations ago, not centuries, not some distant figures in a history textbook. It was against the law for my great-grandfather to name his children after himself and to marry his wife legally.

So when was this period of thriving black families?

It certainly wasn't during slavery, when the idea of the black family by law couldn't even exist.

Was it during Reconstruction, when the first generation could marry legally? I don't think so.

It certainly wasn't in the early or middle twentieth century. I was born in the middle of the twentieth century, and I grew up in a Brooklyn community surrounded by kids who came from single-parent families.

My point here is that I believe we are romanticizing something that was never there. African-Americans haven't degenerated from some golden period of black family unity— because we never had a golden period of black families.

But my further and more important point is this: While we have always had family breakdowns and single-parent family structures, we have always had strong family values. And those values were derived from the black community that surrounded us, not from the existence of a mother and a father in the household at the same time.

My mother, Ada Sharpton, raised me on strong family values with no father in the home; most of my friends in Brooklyn had strong family values and came out of so-called broken homes. I think what Moynihan and a generation of scholars and pundits missed is that we may have come out of broken homes, but we didn't have broken families. We didn't have fathers, we didn't have any means of an adequate existence, we didn't have any kind of comfort level, but we had standards.

My mother raised me so that I was expected to be something, expected to take the strands of opportunity that were presented to me over time and stitch them together into a successful life. So even though my home was broken, I was never broken. I was challenged to live up to my mother's expectations. I say often in speeches that I never knew I was underprivileged until I attended Brooklyn College, because I was never raised to focus on what I wasn't, what I didn't have. I thought I could be great. I thought I could be a minister. I thought I could achieve. I thought I was as good as any of my classmates, because my mother, my pastor, my teachers, the circle that compensated for me coming from a broken home, taught me about great possibilities.

All of that is what has been lost in this generation. We have been sunk by low expectations. We have come to define ourselves, and let others define us, by what we don't have.

When I was growing up, we were intent on challenging the barriers we confronted, not submitting to them. And let me say this again: It had nothing to do with our family structure, whether we had a father in the house, not even with the amount of money our mothers brought home. We would never let somebody get away with telling us we weren't going to make it because we were fatherless. That would have been like spitting in our eyes.

My mother went from owning a new Cadillac every year and living in a private home to becoming a domestic worker after my father left. She would walk to the subway every morning at five or five thirty to go down to Greenwich Village to scrub floors for people, trying to take care of my sister and me and supplement the meager welfare check she would get. Sometimes I would make that walk with her to the subway to make sure she didn't get her pocketbook snatched, and she would talk to me, feeding words into my head that had powerful messages behind them. "You're gonna be somebody," she would tell me. That's family values. This was a woman whose life crumbled, who decided to live for her children and never give up, committing herself to them and their well-being. That's more family values than some rich woman who has a nanny raise her children. So put me up next to a guy who had a daddy and a mommy and a trust fund to take care of all his needs, and he's going to teach me about family values? Did his parents teach him more about family values than my single mother on welfare, getting down on her arthritic knees to scrub floors for me? I think not. I know more about family values than he does, any day of the week.

No one has fought harder than I have in my lifetime against inequality and unfairness. But I've never taught anyone that the inequality and unfairness they might face is an excuse or a justification not to do everything in their power to overcome. Yet somehow, that's the message that has seeped through to the generations that came after mine. We allowed a spirit of dysfunction and surrender to supplant our spirit of determination. While women like my mother made sure that my generation was challenged by what we didn't have, now it seems to define us. Limit us. Break us.

When I give speeches, I sometimes use a helpful analogy:

If I step off the stage and knock you off your seat, that's on me. I've abused you, knocked you to the ground for no reason. But if I come back a week later, and you're still lying on the ground, that's on you. If you're not responsible for being down, you *are* responsible for getting up. But that's not what's happening in our communities and families today. We're not getting back up. We must figure out a way to reenergize and reignite the spirit of get-up in our communities. I am sad and burdened, almost to the point of heartbreak, that we let our young people lose it. We allowed it to slip away in a generation, disappear into a fog of disconnection and self-centered entitlement. When I meet with young people, I see it in their eyes, in their faces, in their demeanors, in their voices. They're telling me, *I ain't gonna be nothing nohow, so why bother? I'll just join a gang, take me out in my twenties. I don't care.*

When things were much worse off, we didn't surrender. We can't accept it now. That is not the legacy of our ancestors. It is not us.

I started to notice the change in the mid-1990s, seeing young people who didn't seem to hear what I was saying to them, who didn't think all the talk about uplift and self-improvement applied to them. Whereas my generation grew up with songs such as "Say It Loud" by James Brown, "What's Going On" by Marvin Gaye, "The Message" by Grandmaster Flash and the Furious Five, and "Fight the Power" by Public Enemy, all records exhorting us to action, by the '90s, that message had started to give way to more self-focused tributes, to weed and sex. It started to become acceptable, even in vogue, to live a thug life. In one of the most damning developments, to young African-Americans, it seemed that blackness became synonymous with thuggery, hood life. It was the definition of what it meant to be black.

I remember how hurt I was when my daughters told me this way of thinking had so permeated young black minds that it was even present on their college campuses. Even in college, if you were well-spoken, well-read, eloquent, you were acting white, they told me. So the converse was that to act black, you were supposed to act like a thug, a street urchin? That's a crippling and racist self-image. But it's been sold, reinforced, and glorified by the last fifteen years of black culture. The music, the movies, and the literature all became a celebration of the thug. So if that's blackness, what does that do to W. E. B. DuBois and James Baldwin and Leontyne Price? They're not black? Or Dr. King—he's not black? What are you talking about? Blackness was never about how low we were; blackness was about no matter how far down they brought us, we found a way to get back up. That's the black legacy—not just to our children but to all of America.

Using the previous analogy, about me stepping off the stage and knocking you off your chair, what we are doing now is getting knocked off the chair, and not only are we not getting back up, but we are lying on the ground and rapping about it.

I'm down . . . bump bump bump . . . I'm down . . . I ain't shit.

It may be entertaining, or even funny, but what kind of damage is it doing to the psyche? What you should be rapping about is, *You knocked me down, but I'm just gonna get right back up.* Or, *Hey, you shouldn't have knocked me down in the first place!* But instead, we're making it fashionable to be down there on the floor, embracing it, making it cool and black to be doing jail time, to have eight kids from eight different baby mamas. I think that's sick.

Please understand, I will always preach that black men must take responsibility for their children. That's something I believe wholeheartedly, especially since I saw in my own life, with my own father, that too many men refuse to take proper responsibility for the care and upkeep of their children. But I have to take exception to this idea that the reason black kids aren't excelling in school is that they aren't reared in a traditional family. I feel as if I would be doing violence to the years of hard work put in by Ada Sharpton to accede to that. This message is especially bothersome at a time when we see the very idea of what is a traditional family transforming before our eyes. It's clear that America needs to update its image of what a family looks like. How do we get sociologists and social commentators trying to instruct America to enlarge the view of a positive family environment, while telling African-Americans that the black community's problem is the lack of traditional families? You can't have it both ways. We have states such as Maryland and Washington deciding that same-sex marriage is legal, and we have gays adopting kids in big numbers—but blacks have to have a mother and a father in the home together in order to thrive? Is that what we're saying here? Because it seems to me that if the contemporary societal message is that the traditional family is not traditional anymore, then please

70

don't use that archetype of the traditional family to beat down African-Americans, particularly black single mothers.

What the black community needs in the current environment is a redefinition of community. We need to reinstitute a place where the teachers are committed to lifting children up and not teaching down to them, where institutions such as the church are dedicated to uplifting kids, where everyone in the community works together to implant in every young person the idea that the community expects success from them. But to count heads on who has a daddy at home at a time when the daddy might actually be another mommy is unfair and counterproductive. If I'm free enough to say people have the right to marry someone of the same sex, then don't come to me wielding that traditional model. American society is feeding blacks a nineteenth-century family photo while giving whites a twenty-first-century liberated view of family. That's not fair, and it's not right.

This doesn't mean we are removing responsibility from the fathers. No, what we are saying is that if you have a child, you are responsible for that child, regardless of your sexual orientation or family type. And to extend it further, if you live in a community with children, you are responsible to help all those children, even if they don't share your DNA. If you're an accountant or a hairdresser, or whatever profession you happen to be in, commit some of your life to teaching, molding, mentoring young people in your community. Your lifestyle choices are your own, but your obligation is to the community and to the children. That means all of us putting aside our ridiculous, self-centered preoccupations and taking care of our children, making sure we create an intellectual climate in which they thrive, which pushes them to reject mediocrity and excuses.

Right now, what is happening in America is exactly the opposite. We are cultivating a climate that celebrates mediocrity, even idiocy. Just fifteen minutes of reality television illustrates everything that's wrong with the American climate—five minutes with Snooki on *Jersey Shore*, five minutes with the ladies of the *Real Housewives* franchise in any of its many cities, and five minutes with Honey Boo Boo and her blissfully ignorant family. These shows and dozens of others provide a virtual dissertation on the modern failings of American culture. The dumber, more ignorant, and more anti-intellectual you are, the quicker your path to stardom. And that's not even including the endless drumbeat of "niggas," "bitches," and "hos" on the radio airwaves.

This enthusiastic American celebration of decadence, debauchery, and ignorance transcends race—we're all there now; no community is immune. In a classic illustration of American inclusiveness, we've even given a vehicle to the Arab community to parade its own unique brand of brainlessness on a reality show called *Shahs of Sunset*. Ah, the beauty of America. Let's show our young people—hell, show the world—how low, irresponsible, undisciplined, and uneducated you can be in this great nation and still get paid.

Our children see the condition of their schools and understand what the society is telling them: You are not important. If you're black, Latino, or poor white, and your school is falling apart—and the fancy public school across town is dripping with amenities—and you're already inundated with videos and music that says you're nothing but a nigga, a bitch, a spic, a ho, what are you supposed to think but that you're nobody? You don't have a sports team, you don't have a pool, you don't even have computers in your classroom.

It all matches the message you're hearing on the radio: *You ain't shit.*

But if each of us looks upon these children as our own, if we consider that we all have a responsibility to not only the young people in our families but also the ones in our neighborhoods, our communities, and across the nation, we will all feel it intimately when children in a particular community are forgotten or disrespected. That should be a requirement for citizenship in this country we profess to love: If you truly love America, you will also love Americans.

10

DON'T GET HYPNOTIZED
BY THE SHINY OBJECTS

I first met James Brown when I was a boy growing up in Hollis, Queens, not far from the big house where Brown lived. The kids on the block would stand by the gate outside his house, which loomed before our young eyes like an urban castle, and wait for him to come out and talk to us. He would tell us the sorts of things that older black people liked to tell kids: "Stay in school" or "Don't do drugs." He'd also say things you were not likely to hear from a lot of other black people at the time, such as "Be proud of being black." He was already a towering figure in the music industry by then, the creator of both funk and soul music, with iconic hits such as "Cold Sweat," "It's a Man's Man's Man's World," "Papa's Got a Brand New Bag," and "Say It Loud—I'm Black and I'm Proud" (a song that many credit for making the African-American community begin to favor the descriptive moniker *black* instead of *Negro*).

The relationship I had with James Brown turned out to be one of the most meaningful associations I've had in my life, one that shaped a lot of what I eventually became.

In 1973, when I was eighteen, James heard about my National Youth Movement and decided he wanted to help me raise money by doing a benefit concert. James seemed to really like me and took me under his wing. He started inviting me to his shows to help out, eventually bringing me all around the world with him and even appointing me as his manager because he knew he could trust me. Our relationship became like father and son. In fact, James's father, Joe Brown, once said I brought out the best in James because he wanted to live up to my admiration of him.

Those years with James were a heady, glorious time for me. I learned a great deal about human nature, about business, about the black community, about the music industry, and I met huge stars in just about every field imaginable.

In fact, James was the one who told me to shorten my name to Al. Up to that point, I was known as Alfred Sharpton.

"Reverend," he said to me one day (he always called me Reverend). "Cut it to Al. You don't need four bars [as in 'Al-fred Sharp-ton']. Just Al Sharpton. Alfred's too much."

If James Brown tells you to shorten your name for the aural benefits, you do it. From that day forward, I was Al Sharpton.

In a profile somebody wrote on me years back, the writer recounted how I was kind of adopted by James Brown when I was eighteen, after his son Teddy died in a car crash. He said this period with Brown defined me, because that's where I got my style and where I learned to deal with the grass roots—the people with backgrounds similar to James's, the marginalized and the dispossessed. But I don't think that's completely accurate. What really defined me during that time was my decision to *leave* James Brown.

During the year and a half that I stayed with James, I was thrown smack into the middle of a teenager's dream: nights in Vegas, parties in Hollywood, shows in London. I was there when he left to perform before the 1974 Ali-Foreman fight, the famous "Rumble in the Jungle." I was nineteen, and I was a player at some of the most intoxicating cultural events of our time. Can you imagine? He was one of the biggest figures in the entertainment industry, and I was his right hand. What more could a kid ask for?

But I wasn't happy. I knew this was not what God intended for me, to be a road manager and assistant for James Brown. There were bigger things in store for me, a path that I needed to begin to walk. That's why I say don't get hypnotized by the shiny objects, the so-called bling. It would have been easy for me to stick around and live large, but it didn't feed my spirit. So I left James and went back to my mother's place in Brownsville, Brooklyn. James couldn't believe it.

"Oh, he'll be back," James told the people around him. "He can't make a living."

I wasn't exactly certain what my purpose was in life, but I knew following James around wasn't it. I dedicated myself to building my National Youth Movement. There were no guarantees, but it's what I had to do.

When I counsel up-and-coming young leaders, I try to get them to practice consequential thinking: If I do this, what is the consequence? It's something my best friend, Dwight McKee, has been saying in my ear for decades. I tell them the two things you have to be most careful of are money and sex. Those are the twin evils, the flagrant, tantalizing mistakes that will bring the media firestorm every time. When you fall in those two areas, everyone's coming after you. I've made mistakes with money—not really doing anything wrong or egregious but not being obsessively careful. I got lax with my recordkeeping and accounting, and the government came along and accused me of unpaid taxes in amounts that exceeded a million dollars. Even if you didn't do anything wrong, you can't say, "To hell with them!" and walk away. The Bible tells us to avoid even the appearance of wrong, so even if you didn't do the things you are being accused of, it becomes a huge distraction.

Huge distractions also come in the form of sex scandals. This is obviously the most lethal trap in public life, the area where a monklike discipline is sometimes required. Yeah, that young lady looks great, but is she worth it? Is it worth you not being able to have the moral authority to stand up and raise issues? What's more important to you, a weekend in Bimini with a young woman or standing up and changing the course of history?

This is a lesson many men and women can relate to: the need for personal discipline when it comes to pleasures of the flesh. It can happen so quickly—a kind smile and a batting of the eyelashes, and the next thing you know, you can wind up in something you can't get out of without causing heartache and pain. It can happen anywhere, everywhere—the church, the entertainment world, professional life, doctors' offices, law firms. In this age of technology, you don't even have to be in the same place to fall into something unseemly. I tell the people around me all the time, whatever you do in life, assume it's public. So the consequential thinking is, weigh what you're doing compared with your destination. If it's going to get in the way of where you're trying to go or how you want to be perceived, then don't do it. And just as important, don't lie to yourself and claim you don't have temptation. That church song says, "Yield not to temptation." So the presumption is that there is going to be temptation. I get tempted every day, but I realize you can't have your cake—success and respectability—and eat it, too. I don't think I need to explain the rest of that saying; you get the picture.

Public life can be lonely. I learned that early on during my days with James. It was probably one of the reasons he liked having me around, companionship that didn't make a lot of demands on him. It's a lesson that has been hammered home for me as I became nationally known. You can't just walk out of your house and go to the movies like everybody else, because people are going to bother you. Walking to the corner becomes a public display. So you tend to withdraw a bit, and there are very few people you can talk to who really understand what it's like, who operate at the same level as you do. That means your circle gets smaller and smaller, the bigger you get. As a result, entertainers, political figures, and athletes may wind up using drugs and having reckless sexual liaisons, among other things, to fill in that loneliness. I saw what happened to James Brown, Jesse Jackson, Michael Jackson. I took them as cautionary tales, warnings about what happens when you get reckless. I loved James Brown like a father, but I saw him getting himself deeper into legal trouble, having bouts with demons like drugs, totally undermining his career and maybe the length of his life.

A big issue becomes, whom are you going to trust? I tell young entertainers all the time, you can go out with some random woman you meet somewhere, some woman you don't really know, and if she's outside your circle of trust, if she doesn't understand the game inside the circle, then after you have your fun, you end up on some website with buck-naked pictures of you sleeping or doing something worse. That's the world we live in now. I've committed myself to talking about this stuff with young people, because a lot of my role models and mentors wouldn't talk to me much about such things. They didn't want to admit that they had flaws. James Brown was one of the few who invested a lot of time in making sure I knew all about his mistakes. He would tell me, "I did this, Rev, and you should never make that mistake." But most of them wanted to look infallible. I think you wind up looking stronger when you can discuss your flaws and then overcome them. If you can't even admit to them, you'll never overcome them.

While I was with James, sometimes I got powerful reminders that I was in the company of one of the most important musical legends of our time. There was one night in Augusta in the early 1970s that stands out for me. I was just a teenager, but even then, I could understand that I had just been granted a peek at something magical. James and I were driving in his van, just the two of us, with him at the wheel—as a New Yorker, I've never learned to drive—down a dark street in the heart of Augusta's black community. Suddenly, James pulled the van over to the side of the road. He was staring across the street at a big church. I could see that it was the United House of Prayer for All People, the Augusta chapter of Daddy Grace's church. Daddy Grace was a charismatic black evangelist and one of the first black religious leaders to put a band in his church.

"You hear that band?" James said to me, pointing up at the church, which was lit up like a Christmas tree and pulsing with the sound of a jamming band.

I nodded.

Smiling, James told me that he learned the beat he later made famous, the half-beat, from listening to the drummer in Daddy Grace's band.

When James said, "I'm on the one!" that's what he was talking about. James took that half-beat out of the church and changed the course of music history.

People would later ask me how I could reconcile growing up in the church with going out on the road with a huge secular music star like James, but it really didn't feel like such a big leap. There was not much difference between James Brown on the road and Mahalia Jackson on the road, other than the genre of the music they were singing. A lot of the rhythms, the bands, and the lifestyles were the same. James would take me out with him on the weekends; Mahalia would take me out on the weekends. It was still hotel, gig, airport, hotel, gig, airport. Same thing. And the people were the same: talented musicians, little formal education, living by their wits. The members of the JBs were the same people as the members of Rev. C. L. Franklin's choir.

Being in the studio with James was like suspending time. I was there when he recorded "It's Too Funky in Here." I was with him in New York when he did "Papa Don't Take No Mess." When James recorded, he would actually dance as if he was onstage. He'd be dripping wet. He was famous for his *Live at the Apollo* recordings, but every recording with him was like a live recording, because he would actually do the spins and all the moves there in the studio. He said he wanted to feel the song while he recorded it. And he'd do it over and over and over again. He had become famous for his demanding, taskmaster ways, and I saw them up close. The more exhausted the band got, the more James said, "We're gonna do it again." You were almost ready to jump out the window of the studio. Over the years, I got to where I just knew that if I got a call at night from James, "Rev, you're going with us to the studio," I was not going to see daylight until about ten the next morning. It was nothing to him to do nine or ten hours in a row. It seemed as if he just enjoyed having me there with him.

When he finished a song, he'd always want to know,

"What do you think? How did you like it? You think it's gonna be a hit?"

To James, every song he did was the best song he'd ever recorded. No matter how many hits he already had, he'd say, "This one is gonna be bigger than anything I ever did. This is the hit. This is the one."

It fascinated me how he would always cut more songs than they were scheduled to do; he'd cut three or four songs that just disappeared into the ether. Maybe four years later, he'd pull one out and say, "Time to put this on the album now." He'd have a sense when he made the recording that it wasn't the right time for the public, but he heard the music, and he heard the words, and he wanted to record it.

One day in 1979, several years after I left him the first time, I got a memorable phone call from James.

"Rev, I think I want to do a gospel-rap record," he said.

"Gospel-rap?" I said, not understanding how those two things could possibly go together.

"Yep. I want you to preach. I'm going to sing. I've never done a gospel song."

But I was still confused. "Me preach and you sing? How's that going to go?"

"Rev, I got this," he said.

So after I flew down to Augusta, we got into his van, and he drove us to a studio in Greenville, South Carolina, driving about ninety miles an hour the whole way. The JBs were already there when we arrived. James liked the James Cleveland song "God Has Smiled on Me," so that's the one we were going to do but reimagined with an up-tempo beat. He taught the band the tempo he wanted. After about two hours, when they finally got it, he started singing, "God has smiled on me . . . He has set me free . . ." And then he pointed at me.

"What?" I said.

"Preach!" he said.

"What am I going to say?"

"Just say it from your heart!"

And so he started it again, then he pointed at me—and I started preaching. He'd break in and start singing again, then he'd point at me to preach again. We did that for hours, recording two or three songs that night, with James, me, and the JBs. James believed in improvising. He didn't read music; he didn't even really read lyrics. He mostly believed in going with what came from the heart. And that's what he wanted me to do. The man was truly a gifted musical talent.

James tried to get those songs out on the market for mass distribution, but he never found a willing partner in the music industry. I still have the recordings, though.

After we made that record, James asked me to stay with him again. His manager at the time had just had a heart attack, and he needed some help keeping the proverbial trains running. He got me a house, and I moved back to Augusta. This was when I began a serious relationship with Kathy, one of his background singers, whom I had met years earlier during my first stint with him. We got married during this time and lived in my house in Augusta. But I woke up one morning and realized I needed to leave James again. I didn't want to be in entertainment. Yes, I was making money. Yes, I was married now and had responsibilities larger than myself. But I wasn't happy. I knew what I was doing just wasn't me.

I brought Kathy back with me to Brooklyn, and we lived in my mother's house for six months. Again, James kept predicting that I would come back because of the money—and he was right; I was broke. But I had fixed it in my mind that I would establish myself in the ministry and by doing activist work. I was constantly being pushed in that direction by invisible forces. I was broke, but I was happy.

A year or two later, on December 22, 1984, a white man named Bernhard Goetz, fearing that he was about to be robbed, opened fire on a group of four black male teenagers on the Number 2 subway train in Manhattan, igniting a blaze of controversy and media scrutiny. To me, the racial connotations were clear. While many were lauding this man as the heroic "Subway Vigilante," I knew I had to call attention to the risks of allowing anyone who perceived danger to open fire on black males. As I began to stage protests in the Goetz case, I started to find my rhythm. My civil rights career was reborn, and I never looked back.

I thought I had permanently left entertainment behind, but the music business wasn't done with me yet. Don King, the biggest boxing promoter in the world, decided that I should become a major concert promoter, working alongside him to become to the music industry what he was to the boxing world. I had worked with King on the Jacksons' Victory Tour in 1984, which King had promoted, and I had helped promote a few other concerts. Even Michael Jackson and James Brown were urging me to do it. But that's not what I wanted to be.

When you know what you want to do, you get to the point where you don't even need guarantees that it's going to work. If you have that conviction, you will turn down guaranteed income, big stacks of dollars that could be very helpful in raising a family, and you will wander down the uncertain path. But I did have one guarantee: I knew I would be happier on that uncertain path.

Over the next decade, I watched as James Brown's half-beat became influential in another music form that was growing like fertile vines in my native New York City: rap music. Rap was a powerful rebellion against a cultural mainstream that was ignoring the pain and deprivation in the inner city. From its first notes, rap became an angry canvas on which these urban geniuses painted their pulsating, lyrical masterpieces. The volatile ethos of rap was captured perfectly by Public Enemy in their seminal song, "Fight the Power." Rap artists at the time were the antithesis of what was accepted in the music world. It was the same way James Brown was seen in his time. Rappers were drawn to the rage and the hope that came through James's music. He became like the patron saint of rap and appears to have been sampled by the rap culture more than any other artist. Songs such as "The Payback" and "Papa's Got a Brand New Bag" all found their way into the belly of rap, woven into beats and melodies like an intricate web of black consciousness and black anger, raging against the cultural and musical establishment. Rap and James came from the same places, the raw soul of black America.

When rap music began, I was still in my early twenties. It was the music of my streets, the music of my generation of young, post-civil-rights African-Americans, impatient for our piece of the American pie. Full Force, Public Enemy, Russell Simmons, Run-D.M.C., those guys were around my age; I identified with them. That's where I got the jogging suits that became a part of my regular outfit. The processed hair came from James Brown, but the clothes were straight from the hip-hop generation. In fact, Public Enemy would come to our rallies at the Slave Theater in Bed-Stuy, joining the "no justice, no Peace" movement, weaving the sentiment into their songs.

I was there at rap's beginnings, and I saw it begin to change. It started to go from a music of rebellion to a music form that was co-opted by the recording industry establishment, which made it more acceptable and less threatening in its lyrics and presentation. I saw the transformation up close. It was a powerful lesson for me about what happens when you let outside forces take control of your culture, when you are so entranced by the dollar signs that you hand the soul of your community over to a corporation. We started with guys who were in touch with the streets, expressing their pain. And we wound up with guys assigned by the corporate music world to be politically nonthreatening, to become in many ways minstrels who would entertain people at their base level and play into stereotypes of blacks—they want to have babies they won't raise, they want shiny jewelry and fancy cars without working for them, they want to call their women "bitches" and "hos."

Understand, my primary complaint was not with the artists. They were the victims. I was fighting against the manipulation of a culture. I saw the musical establishment break, dehumanize, and incarcerate James Brown. I visited him in jail when members of his family wouldn't. I saw them break Michael Jackson, too, and I preached both of their funerals.

The workings of the music industry can't be fully understood until you see it up close. It's why so many artists wind up broke and broken toward the ends of their careers—and, in many cases, at the beginnings of their careers, too. When you step into that den without an intimate knowledge of the game, you will walk out with a chunk of your hide missing.

Once the artists have "made it," the first thing they do is move out of the community. Certainly, you can't fault them for using their new wealth to buy themselves a fabulous new lifestyle. But after they move out, the new norm becomes: Stay away from your people. Don't get politically involved. Don't become community-involved. You see it across the entertainment spectrum, from musical artists to actors to athletes. There was a time when our artists would be deeply involved in political movements, whether it was Max Roach with Malcolm X, Harry Belafonte and Sidney Poitier with Martin Luther King, Public Enemy with me. But now they were being told that the more isolated you are, the more successful you'll be. I felt that I needed to question that

STOP - LOOK
and LISTEN

GOD'S 11 Year Old

Wonder Preacher

Minister

Alfred Sharpton

- will be at -

Pentacostal House of Prayer

Incorporated

203 Nostrand Ave. cor. Pulaski St. B'klyn, N. Y.

Sunday, October 23rd, 1966

at 7:30 P. M., Sharp

Rev. LUTHER DINGLE, Pastor

COME OUT and BRING YOUR CHILDREN
THAT THEY MAY GET A MESSAGE
OF INSPIRATION

Sponsored by the Church Organist Sis. GWENDOLYN DINGLE

ADMISSION A FREE WILL OFFERING

SOUL SAVING

Easter Holy Week Revival

— Conducted by —

GOD'S 17-YR. OLD WONDER BOY PREACHER
MINISTER: ALFRED SHARPTON

BEGINNING EASTER SUNDAY, APRIL 2, 1972
THROUGH FRIDAY NIGHT, APRIL 7, 1972
AT 8:00 P. M., SHARP

COME SEE AND HEAR THIS ANOINTED LAMB OF GOD

CHARITY BAPTIST CHURCH

1515 BEDFORD AVE. (nr. Lincoln Pl.) BROOKLYN, N.Y.

All Are Welcome

REV. E. L. WHARTON, D.D., Minister
REV. ROBERT L. OWENS, Asst. Minister

Marching at the age of 14 on A&P Supermarket in Operation Breadbasket picket line with Reverend William Jones, 1969.

Reverend William Jones (left), my pastor and clergy at my 16th birthday, 1971.

With my mother, Ada Sharpton (right) and neighbor Henrietta Johnson (left) heading to church, early 70's.

Vice President Bush meets with James Brown and myself in the White House, 1982.

Jesse Jackson, Chief Judge Jones and I in 1983 as Jackson prepares to run for President.

Muhammad Ali with music executives at my War on Crack luncheon, 1985.

Painting a red X on a crack house, exposing where crack is sold in our community, 1985.

With Martin Luther King III (left) and Dexter King (right) at the War on Crack dinner, 1985.

With US Senator Al D'Amato and Bishop Frederick Douglas "F.D." Washington, who helped me start preaching at age 4, 1986.

Visiting James Brown in jail, 1990.

Eddie Murphy and I at
Murphy's house, 1991.

With the New Jersey 4 and their legal team, 1998.

Dr. Betty Shabazz, Jesse Jackson, Dominique, Ashley, Kathy and I, 1991.

At the UN with Nelson Mandela and Mayor David Dinkins, 1993.

publicly. It was antithetical to our culture and our history. The lesson is clear: Stay close to your roots. When you don't, when you allow others to pull you far away from the culture, the communities, and the sensibilities that boosted you to your success, you will eventually lose your way.

Artists told me that if they were saying something conscious, something positive, they couldn't get a record deal. The corporate entities were controlling the language to sell more records. So I started questioning why these hip-hop artists would only be allowed to use certain lyrics. When I got involved, some of my friends, such as Russell Simmons, were alarmed. Nobody is more committed to community uplift than Russell Simmons, and I have a lot of admiration for all the causes Russell has gotten involved in.

When I said I didn't appreciate the use of the *n*-word, the *b*-word, and the word *ho* in song after song, Russell told me, "Rev, you can't tell people what to say. We got free speech."

I answered, "Russell, you're right. They got free speech. And so do I."

I have the right to say I don't agree with it. They have the right to say "nigga." I have the right to say we shouldn't be saying that.

It was important for me to make clear that I wasn't coming at this as some churchified saint. I've used the *n*-word—too many of us in our community have used it. And it's wrong. But my problem was with the record companies, more than with the artists. At my organization, the National Action Network, led by Tamika Mallory, who's now the executive director, we started the Decency Initiative, which aimed to "reduce the dialogue of indecency" in the entertainment industry and called for the removal of *nigga*, *bitch*, and *ho* from the industry's lexicon. Right away, I heard the criticisms. "Oh, Sharpton is older now; he doesn't understand." But I understood, all right, and it had nothing to do with age. I understood that most of the guys who started rap were my age, and I understood that the guys running the record companies these artists were working for were actually older than me.

When we met with the record companies, we had some pointed questions: If free speech was the reason they put out records that contained the words *nigger*, *ho*, and *bitch*, then why did they take records out of the stores that were considered anti-Jewish? Or anti-police? Let's get this straight—if something was anti-Semitic, then it was hate? (And I believe that's correct—it is hate, it shouldn't be put out, it's wrong. If it's anti-Italian, or anti-Irish, or anti-gay, that's all hate and shouldn't be put out.) But calling blacks niggas was free speech? Everything was hate speech except when it was directed at us?

Either have no standard, or have a standard for everybody. That's still my problem with the record companies. If *nigger* isn't the anti-black word, then what is it? Let's have a meeting and decide what it is. But there's got to be a word you can't call us if you say there are words you can't call everybody else.

We tried, we pushed, we agitated, but clearly, that battle was lost. So we sit now in the midst of a wave of black music and rap that has only grown stunningly worse, with an inundation of songs that so thoroughly glorify violence and drugs and exploit black women that sometimes I feel embarrassed listening to contemporary black music on the radio for more than a few minutes. We've clearly lost two things: a moral compass and boundaries. What is it that we are trying to suggest culturally to those who buy our art? Is there no line we won't cross? You can call us anything, you can say anything about us? That's not healthy.

Just a few decades earlier, African-Americans owned many of the labels that were putting out black music—such as Berry Gordy at Motown, Al Bell at Stax, and Kenneth Gamble and Leon Huff at Philadelphia International—and African-Americans such as LeBaron Taylor and Jim Tyrrell also held influential positions inside the major white-owned labels. These men would not have permitted today's brand of damaging, exploitative music, because they would have seen it as music to be consumed by their kids. But things have changed drastically in the music world over the last few decades. Now there are just a handful of conglomerates controlling the industry and a tiny number of African-Americans with the power to even sign a deal. Ironically, at a time when African-Americans have made incredible strides in almost every segment of American society, when black music stars such as Jay-Z, Beyoncé, and Rihanna rule the charts, in this industry whose creation significantly bears our fingerprints, we have less power than we had twenty years ago.

One day during the middle of NAN's Decency Initiative, I got a call on my radio show from a young lady who was nineteen. She said, "You know, Reverend Al, I have to confess something to you. When you jumped on the record industry about the use of this language, I said, 'What's he getting on that for? People have the right to entertain themselves with whatever language they want.' But I was in the car this morning driving to work, listening to the radio. A rap song came on, and the rapper called me a ho once, twice, three times. By the time I got to work, he had called me a ho eight times. How many hos I gotta be before I get to work?"

When you become immune to this beat-down, when you get a constant barrage of "ho" and "bitch" being fed to you on a daily basis, it eventually becomes a part of your self-concept. You are entertained by it, but you eventually emulate that in your life. How do I know this? Because James Brown's "Say It Loud—I'm Black and I'm Proud" made me emulate those words in my life. And Aretha Franklin singing "R-E-S-P-E-C-T" made me emulate that in my life. If you take the songs of the times when we were most progressive in our community, there is a correlation. And conversely, if you take the times when we were most regressive, you also see a correlation. We're talking about getting high, scattering babies all over town, just hitting it and keeping it moving. Such music, I believe, is helping to suck the hope out of the people, making them numb to their straits, rather than inspiring them to crawl their way out of the gutter.

When I get into debates about this with the artists, they say they are just a mirror of what's going on in society, in our community. I spoke at Rosa Parks's funeral in 2005, right after I had met with some rappers in Detroit. They said, "Man, why you on us? We understand the history, but we're just a mirror, we reflect what we see."

I said, "That's strange. I use the mirror every morning. I go into the bathroom, look in the mirror, and I see hair all over my head, sleep all in my eyes, slobber all around my mouth. But I don't walk outside and leave it that way, talking about how I'm going to keep it real. No, I clean my face. You use the mirror to correct what you see, not just reflect what you see."

It doesn't take a musical genius to reflect what's there. It takes a genius to correct what's there. That's why in slavery, you wouldn't hear us singing about how we glorified working in the cotton fields. We were singing about "Go down Moses . . . let my people go." That's why in the civil rights days, we weren't singing songs about "Nigger in the Back of the Bus." Or "Ho at the Water Fountain." We were singing "We Shall Overcome." Our culture, our artists, drove us toward where we wanted to go; they weren't just reflecting where we were.

You show me Dr. King marching in the South, I'll show you Mahalia Jackson singing "Amazing Grace," I'll show you James Brown singing "Black and Proud," Sidney Poitier in movies such as *Guess Who's Coming to Dinner* and *They Call Me Mister Tibbs,* James Baldwin writing *The Fire Next Time.* It all corresponded with what was going on with us politically, socially. So the current artists tell me they're just reflecting what's going on in society? Well, we have a black president in the White House. We have a black first lady and two young black girls growing up in the White House—and you're rapping about a ho and a bitch? You're out of sync with the times you're in. We don't have three hos in the White House, so what are you talking about? You ought to be reflecting where we are, but you're not. That's no mirror. You're reflecting where you've been assigned to keep us, but we're not there anymore. So, yes, you have the right to argue with me, but I'm going to fight back. I'm not afraid to fight you, because I am you. You come out of a movement all of us started. Maybe the rest of these leaders are intimidated by you, 'cause you claim you got the streets. But I come out of the streets. I know the streets—and I know you don't have the streets. We always wanted to change the streets, not glorify the streets. That's a huge difference.

And I'm not just going to blame the rappers. That moral compass is broken in many sectors of our community, our society. Our megachurches are operating with a broken compass, preaching luxury, materialism, prosperity, get rich. We don't need pastors to preach to us about having gold-plated chains; we need them to help us go break out of the chains. We don't need diamond-studded shackles. Standing up there and failing to talk about economic justice, about fairness, just telling people to shoot for prosperity? That's not preaching; it's not helping to give people the Word. If the pastor is afraid to deal with the body politic? That's not preaching. Standing up there and ignoring the wars in the Middle East? Not preaching. And worse, telling you that you can get that new Mercedes as long as you bring your son over to the Army induction center to go fight an unjustified war? I tell you, that's jive.

Our artists, our politicians, our preachers must find the courage to stand up and be real leaders. Yes, you're going to get hit from both sides—from the established order and from the dissidents. In fact, that's the only way you know you're effective, if you get hit from the right and from the left. That means you are trying to say something that's not being said. That's what happened to Miles Davis, to James Brown. They got hit by the purists, the guys who never wanted them to get commercial, but they also had to fight the commercial establishment at the same time. That's when you know you're being an innovator. Look at Dr. King, constantly under attack by the black radicals, who said he was a sellout because he would meet with Kennedy and work with Kennedy and Johnson on legislation. Malcolm and Stokely Carmichael and the Black Power crowd always criticized him because he would never embrace the Black Power movement and he wouldn't stop meeting with the establishment. But then again, he was the one leading the marches against the establish-ment. So he was getting hit by the right, calling him a trouble-maker, and hit by the left, calling him a sellout. But you see, forty years later, we hardly know anybody's name but his, because he stood for something.

In 1994, when I went to South Africa for the elections, nobody talked about Nelson Mandela worse than the Pan Africanist Congress (PAC). They called him a sellout for negotiating with President F. W. de Klerk. How could he be dealing with the leader of the apartheid regime? They wanted to kill all the whites, not talk about some kind of reconciliation. But twenty years later, I couldn't name one of those PAC leaders, while Mandela is a living legend. The point is, you have to have the courage to be great. You are going to take hits, but you have to know that you are doing it for a greater cause.

This turn in the music was a constant source of anger and frustration for James at the end of his career. He brought it up nearly every time I called him. I guess he felt a sense of responsibility for the fate of black music, since it was his creativity that had forged so much of what it would become. And he was not pleased by what he had wrought.

At the 2006 national convention for NAN, I decided that I wanted to honor James Brown and Jesse Jackson, two people who had been dominant, pivotal figures in my growth. When I picked up the phone to call James, I was a bit nervous, because I knew James never went to these kinds of events. He had always been a loner, not one to enjoy the chicken-dinner circuit. But when I called him and told him I wanted to honor him, he said, "All right, Rev, for you, I'll come." And he came. He told me that his knees were hurting and asked if I could put him up early so he could cut out. I moved the program around a bit and gave him his award first. He graciously accepted it, and then he left.

About three months later, I got a call from James.

"Rev, remember when you came down when we unveiled the James Brown statue?"

"Yeah," I said, thinking back to that special day in downtown Augusta, after he had gotten out of jail, when we watched them pull the sheet off a statue of him on Broad Street, where he shined shoes growing up. He asked me to speak at the statue dedication, where there was a big crowd of about 3,000 or 4,000. James had whispered in my ear to look across the street. I saw a large statue of some Confederate general. "I bet those Confederate generals never thought they'd be looking across Broad Street at the statue of a black man," he said to me.

"Well, this time, they're going to change the name of the civic center here to James Brown Arena," he continued, shaking me out of the pleasing memory. "Would you come down and do a speech for it?"

I said of course I would. I thought it was only appropriate that Augusta was finally now recognizing his greatness. Right after I got to Augusta, his daughter Deanna called me.

"Dad said you and me have to do all the speaking," she said. "He had dental work, and all his top teeth are out. He said he's not coming."

I was taken aback. "Wait, they're gonna change the arena to his name, and he's not coming? He's got to come."

Two hours later, she called back.

"He said he's coming, but we have to do all the speaking. He doesn't want anybody to see his mouth."

When we got to the arena, the place was packed—live TV, the mayor, all the local dignitaries. Finally, James pulled up and got out, looking sharp as a tack. He had his mouth covered with a red handkerchief, and he walked over to sit in the front row. They introduced me to speak, so I got up and explained to the crowd that James wouldn't be speaking because of his dental work. But he interrupted me by raising his hand.

"Nah, I want to say something," he said from under the handkerchief.

Well, James, who didn't want to speak, got up and spoke for forty-five minutes. He talked about me running for president, how proud he was of me, what I was like at sixteen, what his own legacy was. And then he talked about how disgusted he was by the lyrics in music now. He told the crowd that we've got to clean up the music and get back to family and loving one another. Then he sat down.

When it was time to unveil the new marquee, we walked over together to pull down the cord. There was a reception scheduled afterward, but he said to me, "I'm not going to the reception. I want to take care of my mouth. You go take care of all that, Rev."

As you can imagine, for a singer, an entertainer whose mouth had made him a legend, this particular problem with his teeth really disturbed him. I walked with him to his limousine. He turned around and hugged me.

"Always remember," he said, "I love you."

"I love you," I said back to him.

He got into the car, and it drove off. It was the last time I saw him alive.

Three weeks later, on Christmas Eve, I got one of those haunting phone calls we all dread. I was supposed to be leaving the next day for South Africa. Oprah Winfrey had invited me to go to the opening of her school. My plan was to spend a couple of days in Paris to break up the brutally long seventeen-hour flight. I was going to get up early on Christmas morning and feed the hungry in Harlem, which I do every year, then get on a flight to Paris in the afternoon. Christmas Eve night, the guy who was going to travel with me called and asked if I was packed. I told him, "No, I always pack the morning of the trip so my clothes don't wrinkle up too bad."

Before he hung up, he said, "Sorry to hear about your pop."

"My pop? What are you talking about?"

"James Brown. I just saw on the news that he was in the hospital."

"In the hospital? But I just talked to him."

I checked on him every week and had just spoken to him a few days before.

"Nobody told me he was in the hospital," I said. "It must not be that serious."

I hung up the phone and called his daughter Deanna. She was in Mexico on vacation with her family and didn't know anything about him being in the hospital, either. She said to me the same thing I had just said: "It can't be that serious."

Next, I called his manager, Charles Bobbit, who had been one of James's closest friends for forty years and who always traveled with him.

"Oh, no, we took him to the dentist, and we found out he had some emphysema in his chest," Bobbit said. "We're at the hospital now. He's asleep, or I'd let you talk to him. He's all right."

"All right, let me know if anything comes up," I said.

It was about eleven P.M., so I went on to bed, since I had an early morning, as usual. At about one thirty A.M., my cell phone started ringing. It was being charged in the living room, so I decided not to get up. I thought it was one of my daughters, who always had a contest between the two of them to see who would be first to call me on the major holidays and say "Merry Christmas" or "Happy Thanksgiving" or "Happy Father's Day." But it kept ringing. The person on the other end kept hanging up and calling again. So I went to get my phone and saw that the number was blocked. Again, I thought it was one of my daughters, trying to be funny.

"Hello?" I said, finally answering when it started again.

"Rev? It's Charles Bobbit."

"How you doin', Mr. Bobbit?" I asked him.

"Mr. Brown is gone," he said.

"What do you mean, Mr. Brown is gone?"

"James Brown is dead," he said.

"Huh? I thought you said he was all right!"

"I don't know what happened," he said, his voice drifting away. "He's dead."

I sat down on the couch, not even realizing I had hung up the phone. I convinced myself that I was having a nightmare—nothing I'd just heard or done had been real. But I *was* on the couch. My phone *was* in my hand. I had to call Bobbit back.

"Mr. Bobbit, did you just call me?" I asked him.

"Rev, are you sitting down?" he said. "James Brown, your dad, is dead. You're not having a nightmare. He's gone."

I hung up the phone again, the numbing dread starting slowly to creep through my body. I turned on the television and just sat, blankly, dumbly, my mind in a fog. It was about two in the morning. I sat there for three hours without moving. At about five A.M., the words crawled across the bottom of the screen: "James Brown is dead at age 73." That's when I really started believing it, when the reality of my world without James came crashing down on me. Less than a decade after my dad had walked out on me, James Brown came into my life, about as epic and manly as a father figure could ever get. For nearly thirty-five years, all of my adult life, he had been there for me, a strong, assuring presence, a wise word, a sun-eclipsing superstar. Now he was gone. I later found out that among James's final words to Bobbit were, "Look out for Reverend Sharpton."

I called my traveling companion to let him know my plans had changed. Oprah and South Africa would have to be put aside; I was going to Augusta. I called my secretary and told her to make me a reservation. She asked who was traveling with me. I told her I didn't have time to think about that, so I wasn't taking anybody. And besides, it was Christmas. "You're going alone?" she asked, surprised. I never traveled alone. But I would have to make an exception on Christmas. Besides, I wanted to be by myself while I processed it all. But then I remembered something: my annual Christmas appointment in Harlem.

"Wait, I still want to feed the hungry. He would want me to feed the hungry. So get me a flight to Augusta at about noon, after I go up to Harlem." And that's what I did after James Brown died. I fed the hungry in Harlem. Then I got on a plane to Augusta.

The next three days in my memory are a staggering blur of funerals, sadness, and tears. On Thursday, we had him laid out in state at the Apollo Theater in Harlem, where tens of thousands paid their respects. Then, on Friday, we had a small family funeral in Augusta, and finally, on Saturday, we were going to have his big hometown farewell at the arena that had just been stamped with his name a few weeks earlier. I rode with the body for the entire journey. I was exhausted, physically and emotionally spent. At three in the morning, while I was asleep in an Augusta hotel room, my phone rang, another wee-hour summoning to jar me from my dreams. This time, it was the mortician, Charlie Reid.

"Reverend Sharpton?" he said, his deep Southern accent slowly oozing through my phone.

"Yeah, Mr. Reid. Please don't tell me something's wrong now," I said.

"Nah, nothing's wrong, Reverend Sharpton," he said. "I just wanted you to give me authorization. I just got a call from Michael Jackson."

I could hear the wonder in his voice.

"He's in town, and he wants to come by the funeral home and see the body," he said.

"Michael Jackson? But Michael is in Bahrain."

"Nah, he's here. He wants to come by and see Mr. Brown," Mr. Reid said. "I didn't want to wake the girls up."

I was shaking my head, shocked again by one of Michael's moves. "Yeah, he's authorized. But tell Michael to call me."

"All right, I will, Reverend Sharpton."

I sat there waiting, not able to get back to sleep. An hour passed with no call. An hour and a half. So I called Mr. Reid back.

"Mr. Reid, did Michael come?"

"Yeah, he came," Mr. Reid said. "He sat here a whole hour. He told me I combed James's hair wrong. He took a comb, and he recombed it."

"Wait a minute—he recombed the hair?"

"Yeah, he redid it," Mr. Reed said. "Said I did it wrong. He sat here with the body for an hour."

"Did you tell him to call me?"

"Yeah, he said he was going to call you."

So I called Michael myself and told him he shouldn't leave. I knew Michael well—he'd come and sit with the body and then get out of town.

"One day, you're going to have to reappear in public," I told him.

He had not been in the States and had not been seen in public since his trial, which had ended a year and a half earlier.

"What better time to do it? You came to show your respect to your idol," I continued.

"I'll think about it," he said, and hung up.

Word got out that Michael had been in town, but everyone assumed he was gone. However, the next day, halfway through the funeral at the James Brown Arena, Michael walked in. He came over and sat next to me and the family. The band broke into a memorial tribute to James, playing some of his biggest songs. The band members started motioning for Michael to come join them on the stage.

"Sit there—don't go," I said into Michael's ear.

"What do you mean?" he asked me.

"Don't move," I said.

"Why not?"

"Because you don't want the picture everybody sees the first time you come back and are in public to be of you on the stage boogying and dancing and moonwalking. You came to mourn James. Don't get up there with the band."

"OK," he said, nodding his head. "But I want to see the body one more time."

So we stood up and walked over to the casket. The family all gathered around. Michael leaned over and gave James a tender kiss, saying his final good-bye. When I got up to do the eulogy, I talked in the beginning about Michael, how much he looked up to James and the standard of music they had created. Then I asked Michael to say a few words. This was the statement that went around the world, Michael's reintro-duction to the public.

"James Brown is my greatest inspiration," Michael said. "Ever since I was a small child, no more than six years old, my mother would wake me no matter what time it was, if I was sleeping, no matter what I was doing, to watch the television to see the master at work. And when I saw him move, I was mes-merized. I never saw a performer perform like James Brown. And right then and there, I knew that was what I wanted to do for the rest of my life, because of James Brown. James Brown, I shall miss you, and I love you so much and thank you for everything."

No matter how high he had ascended, Michael never stopped looking up to his inspiration, the man who provided him with the guideposts for his greatness. That's the way it is with our idols—a part of us always sees them perched up high on that pedestal where we place them. Michael became bigger commercially than James ever was, became the King of Pop, but James was always his hero, his guidepost.

Nobody else sitting in the audience at that funeral understood better than Michael the pain that James Brown endured, the pressures that led James to make some of the bad moves in his life. Only people who have walked the same path truly understand each other. As I watched Michael lean down and kiss James in that casket, I knew he understood James's battles with drugs and his battles in his personal life, because Michael understood the pain of going into any city and having tens of thousands of people pay to see you but not to have anybody in your life who you feel really loves you. It is a hauntingly lonely and complex life, one that only a handful of people truly understand. But you have to walk the path to know. I understand the pain of great civil rights leaders trying to do things that are noble but knowing tomorrow's paper is going to call them opportunists and hustlers, knowing they are really giving much more than they'll ever get.

But I also know that this role is the one I signed up for, just as James and Michael knew there would be collateral pain as they strove for greatness. As you watch those who came before you, you gain valuable lessons and insights about what awaits you. It is a necessary exercise for all of us, to understand the price we must pay for the path we choose.

James and Michael were arguably the two individuals who most defined black music, one historically and the other commercially, bringing it to a level of success never before seen. But both of them ended up in the same place, disgraced, one sent to prison and the other fighting prison, both battling the establishment. But both of them always upheld the standard. And that standard, that excellence that emanated from the black church and black culture, that striving to be perfect, is what we need in the current generation of musical artists. It is missing, and its lack is felt like a hole in all of our hearts. That's all I'm saying to these artists: You are better, you have more excellence and genius than these corporate entities making money off you think you have. All they care about is your moneymaking ability. They do not care about your history, your roots, what you leave behind. You are more than a money machine.

Sean "P. Diddy" Combs, another music mogul I've grown close to, is a prime example of the capacity of black artists and music industry professionals to grow and change. I first met Diddy when he was in his early twenties, and he was under fire for his connection to a basketball game at City College in Harlem where nine people had died in a stampede. He had promoted the celebrity game, which was supposed to feature several rap stars playing ball. They tried to scapegoat Diddy, when it was really the irresponsibility of the college and the police that caused the tragedy. So I got other community activists to join me in standing up for him.

He was always ambitious, kind of hot-tempered but smart. He was the most natural brand marketer I ever met. He just knew instinctively how to promote, how to set trends. I saw things in him that reminded me of James and Michael. He was a real innovator. As he got older, we would talk more and more. When he got into trouble with gun charges after he and Jennifer Lopez left a party, and Johnnie Cochran was representing him, Johnnie talked to me about supporting him, which I did. He came to church when I invited him. Over the years, he would always invite me to events such as his famous "White Party" in the Hamptons. What I liked about him was that he always had a sense of community. And the older he got, the more he talked to me, asking my advice about people, about deals he was working on, but it was mostly in passing when we saw each other.

He told me he wanted to do something around voting and started the "Vote or Die" campaign in 2004, the year I ran for president, which registered a huge number of young people. But, more important, it created a spirit in the younger generation that made it cool to vote. I think it changed the attitude of young folks in such a way that it helped Obama win in 2008. That wasn't a venture to add to his riches; it was just his heart, doing what he believed in.

One day in early 2005, much to my dismay, Johnnie Cochran died of a brain tumor. As I was sitting on a platform at Johnnie's funeral at the West Angeles Church of God in Christ in Los Angeles, Diddy looked at me and said, "You know, Johnnie was like my pops. Now he's gone. So you're gonna have to be my pops now."

I joked about being just thirteen or fourteen years older than he was but it still being biologically possible for a man my age to be his father.

"I'm serious," he said.

I looked at him closely. He *was* serious. "All right. Well, when you need me, call me."

When we were leaving the church, he asked me how I was getting back to New York. I told him I was riding with Earl Graves, the publisher of *Black Enterprise*, on Pepsi's corporate plane. Johnnie and I were both on Pepsi's minority advisory board.

"Y'all got another seat?" he asked me.

"But you got your entourage," I said.

"They can fly commercial," he responded.

So he flew back with us, and we talked all the way back across the country. He said, "Tell me about how James Brown did what he did. How did he own radio stations when black folks didn't have anything?" I told him about courage, about standing up and going to the next level. I told him that James Brown went to jail as a kid, but he had to get over his street mentality. I told him about Michael, about the ways he changed the game. And it led to a lot more conversations over the years. Sometimes we won't talk for a month or two, but then, out of nowhere, I'll get a text. It'll say simply, "Pops, call me." He'll want to pick my brain about something

These conversations with Diddy paid off a few years ago, when the activist community got commitments from NBC, General Electric, and Comcast to make investments in the black and Latino communities as they were trying to get government approval for a merger. In addition to adding blacks and Latinos to their boards and agreeing to use black and Latino companies for services such as advertising and legal, they agreed to grant two TV stations to the black community and two to the Latino community. There were at least twenty African-American groups that wanted those stations. So Puffy came to my office and told me he really wanted to do this, to own one of the stations. It was clear he would be a very strong owner, with his business and marketing acumen and all his connections—he was and is hip-hop. But I felt I needed to get real with him for a minute.

"You got to remember, you can't be getting into fights at hip-hop parties," I said to him. "You're not just going to be an artist, you're going to be an owner. You're going to have to sit in front of federal regulators. You're not just going to be *on* TV now, you're going to own the station. That will require a different mentality, a different thought pattern. You got to *be* this."

I said to him, "You can do this, you can do that, but you can't do this *and* that. So you gotta choose. Do you want to be the slickest, hippest, butt-whuppingest dude in the hood, or do you want to be the mogul who has a network that can help transform the hood and make mogul kind of money? You can do both; you got the mentality, the heart, and the courage to do both, but you can't do both of them at the same time. You have to be one or the other. It's your choice—the same choice I had to make."

I told him I wasn't preaching to him, I was sharing with him.

"I had to decide whether I was going to be the caricature, just standing up at the front of every march, or was I going to continue marching but use it to transform, to really make solid change? It may mean I have to be more careful with what I say. It may mean I have to discipline my lifestyle."

"Yeah, you're right, Pops," he said. "But I'm ready. I'm ready."

And that's been our relationship. Now he has the television station, he hired a professional team, and I'm sure he's putting together something that will be fabulous. We talk all the time, and I'm proud of how he has transformed. I've seen situations over the last few years where people tried to provoke him and he wouldn't respond. Not because he's turned soft but because he's really gotten hard. He's determined now to go to the next level, and he's not letting foolishness get in his way. Sometimes in counterculture—and that's what ghetto life is; if the mainstream culture won't let you in, you create an alternative culture—the reverse of the truth starts becoming your reality. So what you call soft in the streets is really hard. It takes a lot more strength to walk away from conflict than it does to indulge the emotions and trade the insults or beat somebody's behind.

But I still have the need, the desire, to try to drive this generation toward a greater understanding, to understand the roots of what it is they call their art form. They need to know the historical antecedents and the moral dynamic from which this all sprang. The contradiction, the soullessness of modern hip-hop, was laid bare by the whole Occupy movement. Artists such as Jay-Z and others were caught out there, ostensibly sitting on the wrong side of the movement, on the wrong side of history.

Here was a movement telling the world that it represented the 99 percent who were being economically oppressed by the richest 1 percent, and the modern incarnation of hip-hop is doing everything it can to be in the 1 percent. Flashing the bling, bragging about your opulence, and conspicuous consumption while your people are suffering. So what the growth of this movement—and the statements made by rappers saying they didn't understand the movement—revealed was that modern hip-hop is not reflecting the times. There's a tragic tension that was uncovered. And if they're not careful, these artists are going to become victimized by that. The people who are buying their music are the ones who are being economically exploited. The artists can't begin to look like the exploiters. Creating a fantasy world in the music is one thing, but they can't also look as if they are trying to embody the exploiters in their real lives. And most important of all, they can't look as if they are oblivious to the exploitation. That is not black music. And it has never been.

The key is not to get too sucked in by the fabulousness that's being offered—in the entertainment business or any other career that might be beckoning to you. Once you let in the bling, get seduced by the opulence or the grand lifestyle, it becomes so easy for you to get lost. The big picture is a distant memory, and pretty soon you don't even remember why you got into the business in the first place. When that happens, you're vulnerable to any dude with a hefty checkbook, asking you to sell your soul.

11

HOW TO BE THE GREATEST

There are lessons, and then there are moments that are so impactful that they sit in your memory forever, frozen in time like an exhibit at the Museum of Natural History. Such was the day in Central Park when Muhammad Ali taught me what it means to push yourself to be the greatest of all time.

I knew some of the guys in the Nation of Islam and through them got to know Muhammad Ali. This was in the mid-'70s, after he had regained his title in Zaire in 1974—a fight I had attended as part of James Brown's entourage. Whenever Ali came through New York, I would spend time with him.

In 1977, Ali was in training for his fight against the hard-hitting Earnie Shavers at Madison Square Garden. It would turn out to be his last fight at the Garden, the fight before he lost the title to Leon Spinks five months later. Ali, then thirty-five, would wake up before dawn to run around the Central Park reservoir, the large, scenic lake that sits in the middle of the park. The one-and-a-half-mile track around the reservoir has been a popular jogging site for celebrities and everyday New Yorkers for years, and it has even been featured in movies.

"I'm going runnin' in the morning, you going with me?" Ali asked me one day.

I nodded eagerly, thrilled to get a chance to "train" with the champ. I was in my early twenties, old enough to think I might be able to keep up with him for a minute.

The next morning, I stumbled out of bed in the wee hours, the night sky still blanketing the city. I put on my sneakers and got on an empty subway train in Brooklyn. I met the champ and his entourage at the Statler Hilton in Midtown, now the Hotel Pennsylvania, across the street from Madison Square Garden. We were whisked up to Central Park, the city streets still relatively quiet.

I noticed that Ali was wearing heavy brogan boots, which I thought odd since we were going running.

"Why are you wearing boots?" I asked him.

"It makes my legs stronger," he said.

He was also coated in Albolene cream, which he told me made him sweat.

"All right, Champ, twenty-two minutes," his trainer, Angelo Dundee, announced.

So Ali started running. And I started running, too. Very quickly, I was behind him, huffing, trying to last as long as I could. He was well ahead of me, but I pushed myself to keep going. By the time the champ had gone around the reservoir about two times, he started clocking Dundee's twenty-two minutes. I was confused.

"We already did fifteen minutes," I said. "Why are you starting the clock now?"

"I train myself to start timing after I'm tired," he explained as we ran. "After I'm spent. 'Cause that's how I make it in the late rounds when all of it is gone. When I don't have any more. I train myself to keep fighting beyond what's easy for me."

Right there, I knew I had heard something important. This was one of the traits that made him a great champion.

I saw that same trait in the studio with James Brown at four in the morning, cutting some of the most important recordings in music history when the band wanted to go back to the hotel. James was never satisfied, always pushing the band to do it one more time.

I saw it with Michael Jackson, practically living in the studio for weeks at a time until his music was exactly where he wanted it.

These were men who had risen to the height of their game, demonstrating to me the discipline and hard work required to get there—and stay there. Of course, they might have had more fun with some fine woman or hanging out all night at a party, but that's not who they were. They were about the sacrifice. They taught me that essential lesson: If you want to ascend to that next level, you have to learn to walk past the many temptations that will be thrown in your path. I kept that thought close at hand later on, when my own celebrity would bring me all kinds of enticing propositions from people who didn't necessarily have my best interests at heart. Walking away was easier for me because of the influence of men like Ali in my life. If you're not willing to make those sacrifices, you're not going to achieve your goal. You might have some fun, but you won't get where you're trying to go.

12

STAY FOCUSED, AND DON'T BE RULED BY YOUR EMOTIONS

Whether it was my search for a father figure or for a clearer idea of how to turn myself into a great civil rights activist, one big lesson I took away from all of the men I followed early in my life was the notion that in order to rise, I had to be focused and intentional and committed to a cause greater than myself. The word *focus* here is key. It's something I believe I was lacking early in my career, when I too often allowed my emotions to control me. That was a mistake I made with one of the cases with which my name became indelibly linked: Tawana Brawley.

If I had it to do over again, there are things I would do differently, knowing what I now know about human nature, about the criminal justice system, about the media. The entirety of the case hinged on whether this young black girl in Upstate New York had been violated, as she said she was, by a white police officer, among others. Sensational stuff, sure, but there's no way I would ever turn my back on a young teenage girl in need, even if her claims were going to turn into an explosive media story. That's just not in my nature. But my first miscalculation was in making the case so personal—us against Robert Abrams, the special prosecutor. The lawyers I was working with and I did a whole lot of name-calling. In these instances, the right approach is to fight the case, not demonize the actors. Because when you allow it to become personal, you take away from the objective. Here's a young lady who says she was violated. Let's deal with the facts, what we know. You can conduct an investigation and try to determine what happened to her, but you can't just ignore it because she said the perpetrators were law enforcement. That's what we feared was happening, that the authorities were automatically dismissing her as a liar.

Years later, when I got involved in the Trayvon Martin case after he was gunned down by George Zimmerman, who still hadn't been arrested, I never once even used the name of the sheriff in Sanford, Florida. That was after years of learning the danger of making it personal. Are you about the issues and getting justice, or are you about the sound bite and the name-calling? Hell, we used to call David Dinkins, who was New York's first black mayor, names. What did that get us? Rudy Giuliani.

But it took time, maturity, and growth for me to transform into the kind of leader who had the discipline to control myself and my emotions. I learned by trial and error, making some painful mistakes along the way.

I'll never forget a poignant moment I had one day with Stokely Carmichael, the former Black Panther who changed his name to Kwame Ture. He had originally been a member of the Student Nonviolent Coordinating Committee (SNCC), participating in the Freedom Rides and working closely with King, but he became more radicalized and moved to the Black Panthers. He was the man credited with popularizing the term *Black Power*. He came by the headquarters for my organization, the National Action Network, in the '90s, a couple of years before his death in 1998, and sat with me to talk.

He said, "You know something, you're following the tradition of Dr. King. I helped start the Black Power movement, but it was a different strand."

"You used to attack Dr. King," I said.

"Yep, called him a bunch of names. You know something? When Dr. King got killed, I went to his funeral, and I cried more than his kids."

"Really? Why did you do that?" I asked.

He said, "Because all them years when we would say it's not about turning the other cheek, it's about Black Power, and you're a Tom, you're an old man, he would just smile and never respond. He never once called us a name. Not once. He said he really loved his people, and sometimes you gotta take it for a bigger cause. I never forgot that."

Here was Stokely Carmichael, who got famous as the antithesis to King, in the end respecting King more than anyone. I actually went back and studied that further. He was right; King never responded to Malcolm, never responded to all the attacks from the more militant blacks. That was a real lesson for me. When I was younger, I was always ready to go at somebody, tit for tat. I considered it an essential part of who I was, part of being a New Yorker. You call me a name? Oh, OK, let's go at it. I used to go on talk shows and argue, fight, cuss, whatever. But at some point, you realize that always engaging in the fight doesn't help your cause. If you're going to be focused on becoming a real leader, you learn that some stuff shouldn't even be dignified with a response. Somebody attacks you with craziness? OK, I'll be all those things you said I am, but you're still going to give justice to Trayvon Martin. OK, I'll be all that, but you're still going to give us this Affordable Care Act. Again, you have to be focused and intentional and committed to a cause greater than yourself. If I'm attacked from the right, with people calling me a radical, my reaction is going to be, "OK, whatever." It's not going to bother me. If I'm attacked from the left—people saying, "You're too close to Obama, you're becoming a part of the system"—my response will be, "OK, got it. But I need to go get this Trayvon Martin case in court." Or, "OK, I heard you, but I need to help the president with health care. Our community is disproportionately impacted by coverage denial because we have so many people with preexisting conditions."

I'm focused because, at the end of the day, when they stretch me out and lay me down, those names I'm being called aren't going to mean anything. They're going to say you either accomplished this or that, or you didn't. And that's where you have to keep your focus. That's running the laps before the twenty-two minutes is even being counted, like Ali. That's staying in the studio all night until it's perfect, like James Brown. I know the difference between great men and famous men, because I've been around great men.

Strangely enough, I think it was a work of fiction that stamped me in the eyes of white people inside and outside of New York, creating a portrait that made them think they understood who I was. That portrait came from the mind of novelist Tom Wolfe and his book *The Bonfire of the Vanities*. Released in 1987, Wolfe's novel featured a character named Rev. Reginald Bacon, who was supposed to be based on me. Bacon was a community organizer who was also exploiting the community and taking money on the side by shaking down elected officials. I think the media and the public "Baconized" me as a way to avoid dealing with the issues of racism and police brutality that I was raising. That was a convenient excuse not to deal with the discomfiting questions, dismissing me as a fraud because of a fictional character in a novel. Talk about laziness.

And if they are going to turn me into Bacon, at least follow it all the way through. If I'm picketing the city officials, like the character in the book, and I'm shaking down city officials, like the character in the book, then ask the question: What is Sharpton getting from city officials? What is Sharpton getting from Mayor Ed Koch, who was my most frequent target at the time? Where is the shakedown? Years later, when the late Mayor Koch came to my fiftieth birthday party after he and I had worked together on an education-related nonprofit program, the mayor was asked how he could work with Al Sharpton, of all people, after the nastiness of all those years, when he used to call me "Al Charlatan" and I called him "Bull Koch."

Koch answered, "Oh, we fought, we disagreed—and still do. But I never felt he was a hypocrite. He never came and asked for anything. He didn't have an ulterior motive, whereas many other leaders would say to me, 'I need this program, I need this day-care center, I need this for my church.'"

I never asked for public funding for anything, so there would be no confusion about my motives. I always raised my own money. So where was the "Bacon"? But over the years, as I got older and gained a better understanding of the inner workings of the media machine—hell, as much as it pains me to admit it, I'm actually a member of the media myself these days!—I understand it now: If you're a young reporter and you want to impress your editor, then you want to go back to the newsroom with "gotchas." You don't want to run back into the newsroom and say, "Hey, do you want to know the real story of Al Sharpton?"

Tawana Brawley came along later in 1987, after the Wolfe book had become a big hit, soon to be made into a movie starring Tom Hanks and Bruce Willis, and that was that. It all became self-fulfilling: Sharpton is a huckster.

One of the most telling revelations of the civil rights work I did in the 1980s and 1990s was how uncomfortable New Yorkers were with the social unrest. For the first time, we brought a Southern kind of civil disobedience movement to New York over a long period of time. This was Malcolm X's town; King and Jesse never brought any campaigns to New York. When we marched in Howard Beach, in Bensonhurst, did the "Days of Outrage" to protest police brutality, this was something the city hadn't ever seen: a sustained movement, jumping on issue after issue, rallying every week, leading nonviolent marches, disrupting the city, shutting down bridges, willingly going to jail. It was new, so the reaction of the media and the public was expected: *This makes us uncomfortable, so we must demonize it*. Even black people were made uncomfortable by all the fuss, because they had never seen it before.

But one of the reasons I was able to keep doing it, despite all the attacks, was that I believed in it, saw it as essential to making the city—my city—more just and fair. I didn't come to New York; I *was* New York. I grew up in Queens and Brooklyn. I knew how to talk to the guys in the street, 'cause I had been talking to them and preaching to them since I was a little boy. Everything I had been doing for the previous twenty years had prepared me to be a civil rights leader in my city. Even though my mother and my siblings and potential mates thought I was crazy, I was doing exactly what I had pictured myself doing. They would say, "Al, how in the hell you gonna build a career doing that?" But I never thought about it that way. Growing up as a boy preacher, I never knew normal. So I never pictured a nine-to-five gig in my future.

In the early '90s, I would have regular meetings at Sylvia's Restaurant in Harlem with two close friends of mine, David Paterson and Greg Meeks. All of us were in our thirties at the time, born within a year of one another, and we were all thinking about where we wanted our careers to take us next. On one particular day, we conducted a little poll on where we saw ourselves headed. It was a pivotal moment for us, because it showed how we were activating the long-term vision that would propel us. We went around the table. David went first. His father, Basil Paterson, is still one of the deans of New York politics, particularly in Harlem, and has served the city in many capacities—state senator, deputy mayor, New York secretary of state, and currently a prominent labor lawyer at the age of eighty-seven. In 1985, David was elected to the state senate, taking the seat once held by his father.

"I think I'm going to be the next David Dinkins, the next black mayor," David said.

Meeks went next. A Harlem kid raised in a housing project, Meeks had already succeeded spectacularly, first as an assistant district attorney and then as a politician; he had just been elected to the state assembly.

"I want to be the next congressman from Queens," he said.

They got around to me. I had already been through the wrenching ordeals of Howard Beach, Bensonhurst, and quite a few other high-profile instances of racial injustice in the city. I had just started my National Action Network to bring some structure to my activism and had recently run for the U.S. Senate in New York. But up to that point, my work had mostly been contained in the city.

"I want to do what Jesse does. I want to be the national civil rights guy," I said.

They seem surprised. "You don't want to hold elective office?" they asked me.

I shook my head. "No, I want to use running for office to drive voters to the polls, to drive policies, get in the debates, help push you guys through. I want to do what Jesse and Adam did."

Fast-forward about seventeen years. We were sitting in another restaurant, this time in downtown New York. David looked over at me.

"Remember our meetings at Sylvia's?" he asked, a smile spreading across his face.

"Yeah," I said, nodding my head. "I remember."

"I think we did it," David said, his smile broader now. "I'm the governor of New York. Meeks is a congressman. And you're the national civil rights guy."

It was a sweet moment. But what was interesting about it was that we all understood our roles, our different talents, and how we could make our contributions. Ultimately, if you're going to be an effective leader, you have to pick a space that's comfortable for you. Because eventually, if you're not comfortable in that space, it's going to show. Either the public is going to sense it, or you're going to do something you shouldn't be doing.

Vision is so essential to any career in any field that it can't be overemphasized. It may seem obvious, but you can't stay on a course to your goal until you've decided on a course. I decided I wanted to be the Jesse Jackson of my generation. Jesse decided before me that he wanted to be the Martin Luther King of his generation. Of course, you wind up bringing all your baggage with you—all your psychological issues, the difficulties of your childhood—but you can develop the strength to carry all of it on your journey, or you can make enough money to have somebody else carry the baggage for you. I have actualized my vision by going through the same routine every morning: doing my prayers, reading the Bible, then practicing visualization where I get an image of where I want to see myself. I have been doing this for years. I visualized myself leading an organization with offices all over the country, even when my office was the payphone booth on the corner of 50th and Broadway. I guess I was even doing it when I was a little kid, preaching to my sister's dolls and pretending they were my congregation.

I never aspired to be a politician. I saw running for office as a way of bringing issues that had been marginalized into the mainstream. It's part of the job of an activist, to place front and center in the public mind issues that the state, the media, and those in power want to keep stashed away in the dark corners. So if you run for high-profile office, you're in the debate, with a guaranteed seat at the table. It becomes much harder for them to keep ignoring your issues. It was a model I got from studying Adam Powell, studying Jesse Jackson. So I ran for U.S. Senate, I ran for mayor, I ran for president. I never ran to win. If I actually wanted to hold office, I could have run for other seats that were more attainable. When I ran for president, I put affirmative action, police misconduct, and racial profiling on the national agenda. These issues never would have been discussed during the campaign, wouldn't have had the chance to become more mainstream, if I hadn't been at the table.

I've heard critics say that I was running as a way to make money—to get matching funds, or to have access to fund-raising—but most of the money I raised for my campaigns I put in myself. In fact, I got in trouble for it; they said I put in too much of my own money, and the campaign had to return it to me. No, the point was exactly what we got out of it: to put issues in the public domain, culminating in 2004 with my speech at the Democratic National Convention.

The other accusation that was leveled at me was that I was just doing it for publicity. I've always been amused by that one, which I've been hearing since the beginning of my career. So I go through all the public conflicts and attacks, get stabbed and almost killed, go through all kinds of legal battles and tax troubles, and then they begrudge me for becoming well known? If after all that trouble, all I'm getting out of it is fame—not an opulent lifestyle, not a life of comfort, just a little bit of name recognition—then I think the public got the best of that deal.

What is a civil rights activist if not someone who is engaged to make a public issue out of something that otherwise would be ignored? So when people accuse me of trying to get publicity, that's exactly right. To accuse an activist of seeking publicity is to mean he is competent. Nobody comes to me for their issue to be buried; they come to me to get the attention of the public. When I go out into the community, when I speak at churches and community events, people are steadily handing me letters and envelopes and asking me to look into their issue. They didn't come to me for me to keep a secret. I think the public doesn't understand the point of an activist's job—these people are hoping I can get their particular injustice into the news cycle.

Although my early days were locked into political and racial battles in New York, when I ran for president in 2004 and began to travel around the country to places I never would have gone, I learned something very important about the soul of America: Whether they are white people in Iowa, Latinos in New Mexico, or black people on the South Side of Chicago, they all want the same things. They want their kids to have a better life than them. They want their schools to work. They want to have a fair and even shot at life. They are not that different. And the more they talked to me, the more people understood that what I wanted for my community was no different from what they wanted. But too often, people wind up talking at each other and not to each other.

I also saw that people in positions of power understood a lot more than they let on, but they were so obsessed with maintaining their power that they were not willing to do what they knew was right. Instead, they did what they felt was right for them and their careers. I was moved by James MacGregor Burns's book *Leadership* when I was a student at Brooklyn College because of his explanation of the difference between transformational leaders and transactional leaders. This formulation is similar to Dr. King's idea of leaders who are thermostats and leaders who are thermometers. I've built my career around trying to be a thermostat. When we started doing massive, disruptive protests over racially motivated killings and police brutality in New York, I was trying to change the temperature in the city. If we took a poll before we went into Howard Beach to protest, we would have fought nothing. Clearly, I've never been in the business of human rights to be popular. That's not what being an activist is about.

A transactional leader will do and say whatever he or she needs to get elected, while a transformational leader tries to change the course of history and make decisions that are moral, just, and right. While Dr. King was fighting against segregation, there were other black leaders at the time who accommodated segregation because they got something out of it. They got elected, but they didn't make society better; they didn't make the black community better. They might even have had long careers, but in the annals of history, their names are long forgotten, no mark made, no legacy left behind.

When I was running, I saw a lot of transactional leaders. Like AM and FM radio, we were on different wavelengths: I'm trying to transform society; they're trying to move up in society. Unless you can block their transactions or affect their transactions, they have no motive to help you transform anything. You don't get their attention until you get in their way.

I wanted to create a twenty-first-century version of what the NAACP and others represented in the twentieth century. That was the thinking behind the National Action Network, which I started in 1991 in New York and built into a national organization over the next two decades. I have tried to use NAN as a vehicle to lift up a new generation of leaders, young people in and out of the ministry who are running NAN chapters across America. I am hoping that in this way, NAN can build a slate of future activists who will innovate in their own style and develop their own way of doing things. Given modern technology and the rapid way we have become one global village, there is a need for new approaches to social activism.

But let's be clear: We will always need activists. As long as there is inequality, you're going to need activists—whether it's race, gender, sexual orientation, or immigration. So even with a black president, even with a black attorney general, Trayvon Martin happens. And when the acquittal of George Zimmerman happened we were on the air live and were able to mobilize within days in over 100 cities because you must be able to respond quickly and never give up the fight no matter the verdict, especially if the broader pursuit of justice has not been achieved. I have chapters across the country; I have paid staff. We don't just jump up and respond when there is a crisis; we work at this every day, meeting with community leaders, solving community problems, working with individuals with issues. Our critics say, "They're just ambulance chasing." I say, "We're not ambulance chasing—we're the ambulance." People call us because they know we'll come. In many of our communities, the ambulance they need might not come.

I want these young future leaders to have the activist passion, but they shouldn't be trying to imitate me. My style is completely different from Reverend Jones's or Reverend Jackson's, but their style was different from Martin Luther King's. I tell them, "Respect me, but don't imitate me."

One of the things I have found disheartening throughout my career is the sexism in the upper echelons of leadership, particularly in the black community. The executive director of NAN is a young woman named Tamika Mallory, an extremely talented leader who grew up in the organization from the age of twelve. When I made her executive director, people thought I had lost my mind. People would continue to ask me, "When are you going to choose a successor?" As if it had never crossed their minds that Tamika could be my heir apparent. In addition to Tamika, I have many chapter leaders who are women. But it often feels as if I'm fighting sexism and racism at the same time.

I don't think we've had an honest discussion about misogyny in the black community. I don't think we've talked about the latent feelings of hostility many black men have toward black women, a misguided sentiment that black women somehow have taken part in society's emasculation of black men. Maybe at some point back in our history, black women were used to emasculate us, but if so, they were being used against their will. They can't keep paying for that. And black male insecurity cannot continue to be the justification for asking black women to step back and let some insecure boys play out their manhood issues.

It all brings to mind the battles I had when I was eighteen and was made the youth director of Shirley Chisholm's presidential campaign in 1972. It was the first year that I would be eligible to vote, and I was so excited about the whole campaign and my role in it. Chisholm had been the first African-American woman elected to Congress in 1968, representing the twelfth congressional district in Brooklyn. Chisholm was fierce, brilliant, and courageous. I was proud to be in charge of organizing young people in support of her presidential campaign. But that sentiment wasn't shared among the black leadership. Chisholm said that during her legislative career, she faced much more discrimination because she was a woman than because she was black. I can definitely attest to that, because I saw it with my own eyes.

I attended the unprecedented gathering of black leaders and activists that happened that year in Gary, Indiana, and I was shocked that they would not endorse Chisholm. Jesse Jackson and the others were going with George McGovern. I think a lot of their problem with her was because they felt, *Shirley's into that feminism.* But my response was, *Well, wait a minute, Shirley's a black candidate with our agenda, in addition to a feminist agenda. Why can't we support her?* Shirley lived in Brooklyn, and I knew her very well. I saw the hurt and pain she went through having to fight black men. Shirley was more gifted and courageous than most of her contemporaries, but because she was a woman, she was denied a loftier status.

As her youth director, I felt the tensions. For a lot of these leaders, it was the first time I openly went against them. It was eye-opening, and it was painful, because I had to make a personal choice. I looked up to them, and I couldn't believe their view was that limited and that biased. There's no other way to put it. I knew there was considerable sexism in the church community, after watching the battles Bishop Washington had gone through for his progressive views, such as ordaining women as preachers in the church. But I thought the leaders with whom I was mingling at the convention were more learned than that, more advanced than that. I learned a great deal during those days in Gary, lessons that helped me understand my community over the decades.

Forty years later, we are still going through these gender trials. We have quite a few prominent elected officials who are women, but I would expect the proportion to be greater than it is. So I frequently make conscious decisions in my sphere of influence to ensure that I include as many women as possible in the mix when it is time to establish the leaders of my organization. Of course, it is talent that is my top priority. That was surely the case with Tamika. But I also want to make sure women aren't being discriminated against.

After my two daughters were born, I was even more disturbed by the prevalence of sexism I still saw around me. I've spent most of my life breaking down racial barriers, but it would be the ultimate irony if my daughters were denied opportunity not because of their race but because of their gender. My daughters went to very good schools; I was able to work hard and enable them to have a good education. But if they can't pull up to the table with the men of their generation, having a better education and better training than I had, then I have not done all I was supposed to do by dealing with race and not fighting hard enough against gender bias. My own bloodlines will be carried by two women who will have to deal with sexism and racism for the rest of their lives. It is my fervent prayer that the world they grow up in will see the shortsightedness of sexism, will see how much more powerful and dynamic we become when we grant the seeds of opportunity to every one of us. I hope my daughters in their lifetimes see the day when they can pull up a chair to the table and the man sitting next to them won't find it necessary to make a mental note of their gender. And I say to all the young men out there who might find themselves one day sitting at the table next to my daughters and all the sisters of their generation and the generations after them: Their presence strengthens you, makes you stronger and smarter and more capable. It doesn't diminish you.

13

PRACTICE WHAT YOU PREACH

My social activism is my religion in practice. It is the daily embodiment of my lifelong service to God. As a Christian, as a man of the cloth, I am required to fight on behalf of those who have been wronged, on behalf of the downtrodden, on behalf of those facing injustice. That is my ministry. I don't have a problem with ministers who build cathedrals—maybe that's their calling. But my calling was to fight for those the Bible calls rejected stones. As the Bible says, Jesus was the stone rejected by the builders who became the cornerstone. I feel this intensely because I was a rejected stone myself in many ways when I was growing up.

My activism and its inherent dangers brought me one of the greatest tests that my faith has ever had to endure. It began amid the ugliness of our protest marches in Bensonhurst, a working-class Italian neighborhood in Brooklyn, not far from Coney Island. Sixteen-year-old Yusuf Hawkins had been shot twice in the heart in cold-blooded murder by a racist mob, upset that Yusuf and his friends were in their neighborhood. The mob thought Yusuf and his friends were linked to a neighborhood girl who had been bragging about dating a black man who was going to bring *his* black friends to the neighborhood to confront the young Italians. After the murder of Yusuf, we marched to assert the right of African-Americans to travel anywhere we wanted in our city, particularly after the same thing had happened in Howard Beach, another Italian neighborhood where another young black man, Michael Griffith, age twenty-four, had been killed by a racist mob in 1986. We also marched to ensure that the Brooklyn courts convicted each of the young white kids who were part of the mob that killed Yusuf, which was starting to look less likely. Right after the shooting happened, we marched to persuade the community to give up the identities of the shooters. During the weekly marches, we faced a revolting horde of racial hatred, with the residents of this neighborhood—mothers, brothers, grandfathers, sisters—crowding the sidewalks as we walked through, hurling the word *nigger* and its every variation while holding aloft bananas and watermelons and throwing garbage at us. While the civil rights struggles of the South and the hatred and brutality encountered on the Freedom Rides in Alabama and Mississippi—when activists like the young John Lewis, now the distinguished longtime congressman from Georgia, got beaten and bloodied—have certainly been well documented, I'm not sure that people realize the extent of the vicious racism we encountered up North in places like Bensonhurst and Howard Beach.

One of our lawyers got a call one day from Charles Hynes, the Brooklyn district attorney, who had won election to that post largely because of the fame he garnered as the special prosecutor in the Howard Beach racial killing. Hynes let us know about something the government had picked up on a wire installed inside a social club in Bensonhurst with suspected mob ties.

On the bug, the government heard these mobsters talking about killing me, so Hynes wanted to put me under police protection. Apparently, one of the guys who shot Yusuf had mob ties, and I was bringing the national press to their neighborhood on a weekly basis, which was affecting their ability to conduct their illicit activities such as drugs and numbers running. I had seen enough mob movies to know Rule Number 1: Don't mess with the cash flow.

I'm not going to lie and tell you I was Superman jumping out of my suit into a cape, ready to go take on the scary mobsters. No, I had to seriously wrestle with it. I was just thirty-six, I had two very young kids at the time, and I had really no income. I made money where I could, preaching, and occasionally, folks like James Brown would help us out, but there was no steady income and no big trust fund to support my family if I was gone. I had been preaching about faith since I was a little boy, standing up on that podium and telling my people they needed to trust God to protect them if they were doing right by Him. Now I had to decide whether I was ready to step back out there on those Bensonhurst streets, knowing it could end at any moment. *Now we're going to see, Sharpton, if you really believe in God, if you really have faith.* I said we had to go, keep marching. I believed too strongly in the rightness of our cause to stop because of a threat. After they couldn't persuade me to stop the march, the authorities begged me to wear a bulletproof vest. But I didn't want to succumb to the fear.

Normally, when we do these marches, everybody is trying to get around me, almost knocking me down, so they can get into the camera shots. But the next time we went out there after the threat, no one wanted to stand next to me. We marched for several more weeks without incident—aside from the vicious hatred—so I began to allow myself to relax a little.

On January 12, 1991, we went to Bensonhurst for a march, the twenty-ninth week we had done so, starting the weekend after Yusuf was killed. We pulled into the schoolyard where we usually gathered. The police always cordoned it off to keep the hate crowds away from us while we set up. Usually, they would line us up and form two walls of police protection, one on each side, so that there would be officers on each side to protect us. I was in the car with Moses Stewart, Yusuf's father, who by then had joined NAN. When someone tapped on the window and said we were ready to go, Moses and I got out of the car and headed toward the front of the line to lead the marchers. This was called the "frozen zone" because only police were allowed in the area. As I was walking to the front, I felt somebody brush past me. I said to myself, *Damn, that cop just punched me in the chest!* The guy had on a blue jacket—blue was the color of the day for the undercover cops, so I figured he was a cop. Out of the corner of my eye, I noticed something and looked down to see I had a knife sticking out of my chest. By instinct, I grabbed the knife and pulled it out. When the cold air— remember, it was mid-January—hit the wound, I went down in pain. People started screaming when they saw the blood gushing out of my chest, and they yelled for an ambulance. But even though this was a potentially violent protest march and there were a couple of hundred police officers, there was no ambulance. A quick-thinking fellow protester threw me in the back of his car and said he would drive me to the hospital. One of the police captains told an officer to drive the car, and the officer responded by saying, "Wow, this is my first day on the job!"

I thought, *Not only are they killing me* (I still thought it was a police officer who had stabbed me), *they're gonna give me a rookie cop!* As a matter of fact, I would later file a lawsuit against the city for police negligence in allowing me to get stabbed. The case was settled out of court in 2003.

The wound was more than three inches deep, very close to my heart, and they had to operate immediately to drain my lungs because they were filling with blood.

As I lay there that night, I made up my mind that if I was going to die, I had no regrets about the decisions I had made. I wasn't trying to barter with God, wasn't saying, *If you bring me through this, I'll never do it again.* No, I told myself that if I survived, I was going right back to Bensonhurst and continuing to march. And that's what I did, after getting out of the hospital four days later.

That's what religion is, in my mind: living by what you say.

I had faced trumped-up tax charges in the late 1980s, sixty-seven counts of tax evasion. But I never doubted that I was standing up for what I believed in, and I got acquitted on all counts. I spent ninety days in jail for protesting in Vieques, but I never regretted the decision to fly down to Puerto Rico and trespass on the Navy base where the bombing exercises were harming Puerto Rican children. I once was set up by the government, and they tried to sting me in a drug deal and then leak to the press that I was a government informant—when in actuality, they had tried to pressure me into giving them information on Don King, and I refused. Their decision to leak that false information could have gotten me killed. So I have been seriously tested in what I believe over the years. I'm not some theologian speaking about religion from on high, spouting theories on homiletics from some ivory tower. I have lived my religion down on the ground, in the streets, in hard situations, where your faith is really tested.

My faith got another difficult test when the man who stabbed me, Michael Riccardi, went on trial. For the longest time, I tried not to think much about the incident. My attitude was, *I'm glad I survived it, everything's OK, let's move on.* But more than a year after the incident, I read in the newspaper that he was going to trial, and I got more details about this twenty-eight-year-old man's life. He wasn't in the mob, as we had suspected, but was just a troubled guy with an alcohol problem, who came from a family with alcohol problems. I thought about how the press was condemning this guy, this white maniac who almost killed Sharpton. And I thought to myself, *Wow, how self-righteous are they?* They were the ones calling me a rabble-rouser, a troublemaker, not so subtly suggesting that we would all be better off if I went away. Now they had scrambled up onto their moral high horse and were attacking Riccardi?

In Dr. King's writings, he talks about the ability to forgive and borrows heavily from Gandhi, and I realized that change has to begin with you—you must become the change that you seek. So one morning, it came to me: I had to forgive Riccardi. I had come to terms with my faith after the stabbing, but I had never come to terms with how I felt about this guy. So I called my attorney Michael Hardy, who is also the general counsel of NAN, and I told him to call the district attorney, because I wanted to testify at the trial of Michael Riccardi.

I got on the stand and recounted what I remembered of that day. Then I asked the judge if I could say something to the court and to the defendant. I told the court I was amazed at how everyone was condemning him when all he did was carry out what they told him.

"He might have hit me with the blade, but everybody put the knife in his hand," I said.

I told the court I would like to forgive him; I looked at him and said I wanted him to know I held no ill feelings toward him. Then I got up and left the courtroom. As soon as I had done it, I felt better. After he was convicted and they set a sentencing date, I knew my job wasn't complete unless I went back. I told the judge I hoped the court would be lenient in the sentencing, knowing I had forgiven him. The judge, Francis X.

Egitto, called my statement "noble," but he said what Riccardi had done was "a willful act," slipping past 200 police officers to plunge the knife into my chest, so leniency wasn't the answer. The judge gave him five to fifteen years and said, "This violence has got to stop."

A short time later, I received a letter from Riccardi, which he had written to me from jail. Riccardi said, "I want you to know, Rev. Sharpton, that I grew up with alcohol problems, I had an abusive father, and it occurred to me when I sat in that Brooklyn courtroom that you were probably the first person in my life that ever stood up for me. I just want to thank you. I hope you don't mind me writing you, and I hope your children will one day forgive me for almost killing their father."

The letter really moved me, so much so that I decided to visit him in jail. As you can imagine, the people around me thought I had lost my mind: "Why is he forgiving this white man? Why is he giving away a just situation, when we spend all this time fighting injustice? Isn't this what we want?"

Walking into that visiting room and looking eye-to-eye at the man who had tried to take me out was one of the hardest things I've ever done—harder than recovering from the stabbing, harder than the ninety days in jail after Vieques, harder than testifying at Riccardi's trial. I had allowed Jack Newfield, who was a columnist for the *New York Post* at the time and one of my biggest critics in the media, to come with me. So the two of us walked into the visiting-room cell and sat down with Riccardi. I felt that if I could pass that test, it would bring me to another level in my religious understanding. When they brought him in and he sat across from me, I searched my soul and realized I had no hate, no ill will toward him. He apologized again for stabbing me, and I told him I accepted his apology. Then he said to me, "Why do people call you anti-white? I'm a white man, and you not only went to court for me, you asked the court for leniency."

I said, "Every civil rights leader, every leader in my tradition, they're going to be distorted. That's part of the burden of leadership."

"Well, I just really want to thank you for what you did for me," he said. "Even though I'm doing time, it makes me feel better knowing you forgave me and I was wrong."

"Thank you, but I have to be honest," I told him. "I didn't do this for you, I did it for me. Because I had to know that I really believed what I preached. So this has nothing to do with Michael Riccardi—this has to do with Al Sharpton dealing with Al Sharpton. 'Cause I've said things and done things I shouldn't have said and done. I'm not nearly as bad as the press tries to play me to be, but there are situations where I shouldn't have gone over the line verbally or shouldn't have tolerated others doing it in my presence. I had to do this for me."

That, to me, is the practice of religion. Taking that step out there on faith, even when those around you are screaming so loudly their veins are showing. Belief is when you do what may or may not be popular, but you do it because you know it's right. When I came out for marriage equality for gays, it was right. It's not what we preach in the Baptist church or the Pentecostal church, but it's right. With a woman's right to choose, I may never advise my daughters to get an abortion, but I'm not going to make them do something just because it is my will, so why would I make it unlawful for somebody else's daughter?

I believe strongly in my daily religious rituals. They focus me and strengthen me. The first thing I do when I get up every morning is wash my face; then I get down on my knees and pray. That's what I grew up doing; I believe you should bow to God. Next, I read the 37th Psalm, which is my favorite Psalm, to focus me for the day. Then I read the fourth chapter of Philippians, which talks about how God will give you peace before all understanding, and that sets my tone before I go work out and read the e-mails on my BlackBerry. I say another prayer before I go to bed at night, no matter how late it happens to be, no matter where I happen to be laying my head.

But having gone through all of that, I do not believe I have the right to impose my sincere lifelong beliefs on anybody else. There's probably no pastor in the country who preaches more than I do—every Sunday, I'm preaching somewhere, sometimes three Sunday sermons in three different churches. I might preach in the morning in Dallas and in the evening in Indianapolis. That's the way I always envisioned having the most impact, patterned after the approach of Dr. King and Reverend Jackson. If you pastor one church, you are talking to the same people every week; if you take the traveling-pastor approach, you can reach a different congregation every week.

My point is that I am as solid and steadfast in my religious beliefs as any right-wing zealot or Islamic extremist. I believe it, I preach it, I live it. But I believe that my job as a preacher is to convert people, not compel them. That's what a good preacher does: use the power of ideas, of faith, of love, to draw people to your philosophy and the vision of your savior. This idea that you have to make people follow your beliefs is not only undemocratic, it is an insult to those who really believe in God. Jesus gave people a choice, Muhammad gave people a choice, Buddha gave people a choice. There should be no religion that needs the government to force people to practice it; only the insecure and the insincere need to impose their edicts on the people. It disturbs me how steadily we all seem to be moving in that direction—nations in the Middle East requiring women to dress a certain way in order to be seen in public, states in the Bible Belt of the United States deciding that women don't have the right to decide what they're going to do with their own bodies or that gays don't have the right to build families and give their partners the same legal rights over assets, resources, and estates as everyone else. And all of this done in the name of religion. To me, it is a perversion of religion. I may disagree with your choices, but I'm going to fight for you to have the choice.

I think religion is not what you preach but what you practice. I started preaching before I could read. I've heard some of the greatest preachers in the world, so I'm not impressed by orators and pulpiteers. What impresses me is action, preachers whose religion compels them to action.

My faith and my belief in what it represents sometimes has put me in opposition to other powerful preachers, proving that the practice of religion is an individual act, dictated by your own relationship with your God. In New York City, the exclusion of gays from the annual St. Patrick's Day Parade provides an annual bout of public hand-wringing and a litmus test for the city on the evolution of local politicians and religious leaders regarding the rights of gays. Every year, I would join the gay and lesbian activists who would march in protest of their exclusion. In 1998, I had occasion to come together with John Cardinal O'Connor, the archbishop of New York, for a relief effort by the religious community to benefit Haiti after a devastating hurricane. At the end of the meeting, the cardinal asked if he could speak to me privately, so we went into his office at the archdiocese on First Avenue.

"Let me ask you a question," he said after we sat down. "You and I have always had a respectful relationship. Anytime you wanted to meet, I'd meet you. We always were able to agree to disagree about issues where we had disagreements."

He reminded me of how he supported me after I got stabbed in Bensonhurst and forgave the assailant. O'Connor wrote an admiring column in the *Catholic Digest* about my granting of forgiveness. I wondered where he was going with this.

He paused dramatically. "Why do you march with the gays on St. Patrick's Day?" he asked.

"Because I think they have a right to march on a day that honors their nationality," I said.

"But we're members of the cloth. We preach that the Bible forbids it. We preach that they are going to hell."

"There are different interpretations of that," I said. "But

let's say you're right. Whether I agree with you or not, if they're going to hell, I'm going to fight for them to have the right to get there. They have the right to choose. God gave you a right to choose with a heaven and a hell. What gives you the right to say somebody's got to choose heaven, in your theological understanding?"

He studied me for a moment. "I've never heard it put that way. Let's just agree to disagree," he said, rising from his chair. He extended his hand, and we shook and said good-bye.

When I was tested after my stabbing, my faith and the daily practice of my religion led me to forgive the man who had harmed me. It was a powerful test for me, one that let me know my faith was more than an abstract idea, more than daily habits that one does without thinking. No, it was a real, living, powerful thing. God asks us to forgive others as He forgives us for our many trespasses. While it is not easy, in many ways counter to our natural human impulses, I have found that forgiveness is deeply cleansing, fortifying, even healing. And it is absolutely necessary for growth and maturity. We all hold on to things that we should let go of. You probably have something inside you now that needs to be freed, some slight or offense against you or even some major act that caused you great harm that you are clutching too close to your heart. Whom do you need to forgive?

14

AT YOUR LOWEST POINT, YOU
MAY FIND YOUR GREATEST GIFT

Reaching outside the African-American community to broaden my perspective has been an important element in my transformation and growth in the past two decades as a human rights activist.

In the Brooklyn neighborhood where I grew up, I was surrounded by immigrants. Haitians, Jamaicans, Trinidadians, Dominicans, Nigerians, Senegalese—you couldn't walk down the street without tripping over interesting folks, and interesting foods, from across the globe. Like everybody else in America, these people were striving to work hard, send their children to the best schools possible, and trying to grab their little piece of that elusive American dream.

So when the issue of immigration began to emerge as an explosive political football, my thoughts would drift back to the streets of Brooklyn. These were real people—people who were a part of me. For me, it could never be *them* against *us*. My upbringing undoubtedly compelled me over the years to be naturally inclined to fight for immigrants' rights and to try as much as possible to build coalitions between African-Americans and the immigrant community, understanding that our plights in America were intertwined, particularly as the government moved toward increased racial profiling to enforce its repressive immigration policies.

Of course, for too many Americans, fed a steady stream of threatening media images, the word *immigrant* conjures visions of frightened Mexicans scurrying across the dusty Arizona desert, hoping to slip unseen into American society and immediately become a drain on the American pocketbook. That's become the handy American archetype. You can hardly hear the word *immigrant* without first being accosted by the word *illegal*. In a country founded by immigrants, the ultimate irony is that America has now permanently attached the disturbing descriptor *illegal* to the word that defined our ancestors.

Immigrant. It didn't use to be a dirty word, not when the shiploads came into Ellis Island on those steamers from Europe, blessed by the words of poet Emma Lazarus on the Statue of Liberty: "Give me your tired, your poor, your huddled masses yearning to breathe free, the wretched refuse of your teeming shore. Send these, the homeless, tempest-tost to me, I lift my lamp beside the golden door!"

I can't help but note, as many others have before me, that this country didn't have an "immigration problem" until the immigrants became overwhelmingly black and brown. In 1960, the top five countries sending immigrants to the United States were Italy, Germany, Canada, the United Kingdom, and Poland. I don't recall presidential candidates back then being forced to come up with a stance on Italian, German, or Canadian immigrants.

But by 1970, Mexico had entered the top five. By 2000, when immigration had become an explosive third rail of American politics and there was talk of building electrified fences along the southern border, the top five looked very different: Mexico, India, China, the Philippines, and Cuba. It's not difficult to see the difference between the two lists.

Dr. King was a giant of the civil rights movement, but let us not forget the courageous work of Cesar Chavez, who adopted some of the nonviolent tactics of Dr. King to fight on behalf of migrant farmworkers. With boycotts, strikes, and the creation of the United Farm Workers union, Chavez awoke the world to the exploitation of Latino farmworkers in the Southwest. King and Chavez were also friends and associates who understood the common purposes of their struggle for human rights for black and brown Americans. What happened to the spiritual bond formed by these two great leaders?

I have been disturbed by how quickly forces in the African-American community have succumbed to brainwashing, to wrongheaded propaganda about this issue. When I hear black people repeating this nonsense, saying, "They're taking our jobs," my first response is to ask, "What jobs?" Ever since there have been labor statistics recorded in this country, blacks have been doubly unemployed; our rate has always been double the national rate. The only time black people had full employment in the United States was during slavery—and we didn't get paid. So who was taking our jobs before we had an influx of Mexicans over the past thirty-five or forty years? This country has never intended for blacks to be fully and gainfully employed, and that has nothing to do with Mexicans. So let's stop the blame game and try to focus on the big picture here.

I was thinking about the need for me to move outside of my comfort zone when I made the decision to join my Puerto Rican brothers and sisters in their protests against the U.S. Navy's bombing in Vieques, a small island next to Puerto Rico. I was trying to reach out, to grow, and in the process, I stumbled into one of the most difficult ordeals that I've had in my career. I wound up spending three months in jail because of the Vieques protests. Although it was a harrowing ordeal, that time also turned out to be incredibly important to me, giving me an opportunity to do some serious introspection and planning. I would be a totally different person and a different leader today had I not gone through the Vieques experience. It was surely one of the most impactful three months of my life, setting the stage for much that was to come later.

It all started on a Saturday morning in 2001, when I was riding down the FDR Drive in Manhattan on my way to one of the NAN's regular Saturday-morning rallies. On the radio, they were talking about Robert Kennedy Jr. and Dennis Rivera, a labor leader, going to jail in Vieques. Rivera had gone to jail with me during our "Days of Outrage" protests against police brutality in New York. I was inspired in that instant to respond in kind in Vieques and to demonstrate the viability of a black-brown coalition. I called Roberto Ramirez, a Bronx political leader who was active in the anti-Vieques movement, and told him that I wanted to support them the way they supported me during our protests.

So I got on a plane and journeyed down to the island paradise of Puerto Rico with three influential Latino leaders: Ramirez; Adolfo Carrión Jr., a city councilman from the Bronx who eventually became Bronx borough president and then an official in the Obama administration; and Assemblyman José Rivera, who was also from the Bronx. The way you staged a protest at Vieques was to crawl through an opening in the fence at the Navy base. It was considered trespassing on federal property, an act of civil disobedience. As planned, we were arrested, attracting a great deal of media attention in Puerto Rico and back in New York.

I've been arrested dozens of times on the mainland, so I was expecting the usual court appearance and slap on the wrist. But the way we were treated right after the arrest should have been my first warning that this one was going to be different from the others.

First, we were handcuffed and hustled to a cavernous old jailhouse on Vieques that looked like a castle. We were stripped naked—in front of one another—and searched, as if the four of us had suddenly turned into despised enemies of the state. They put us in inmate clothing and marched us onto a barge with other prisoners to make the trip to mainland Puerto Rico.

On this barge, we were chained to the floor, alongside a row of tanks and trucks that were making the trip with us. Suddenly, on a day that had started out with a peaceful protest in a gorgeous island paradise, I found myself chained to the bowels of a barge, as if it was 1801 instead of 2001 and I was traveling the Middle Passage.

The fifty-eight-mile trip from mainland Puerto Rico to Vieques had taken less than a half hour by air; by barge, that little jaunt turned into a three-hour ordeal. Near us on the barge were several large military trucks that also were being transported back to the mainland. And during the whole of the three hours, as sea water sprayed up into my face and I was helpless to wipe it away, my mind was stuck like a broken record on just one thought as I stared up at a huge truck bouncing around nearby. Was the chain that was supposed to be holding that truck in place suddenly going to succumb to the bouncing waves and allow the truck to crush me to death? There was very little conversation among the four of us. I think they were thinking about that truck, too. This was not the way I had planned for this trip to go down. I sent up some earnest prayers on that barge. I could see the *New York Post* headline: "Sharpton Suffers Death by Truck."

By the time we reached San Juan, we had lost quite a bit of our swagger. But we received a lift when we finally got to the federal penitentiary at about midnight. When we walked into that processing room, a big cheer went up for us from all the grateful Puerto Ricans, thankful that we cared enough about them to put our freedom and safety on the line. They had been fighting the Navy for years, claiming that the military exercises and bombing being conducted on the island were causing cancer and asthma in their kids. Two years earlier, a security guard had been killed by a bomb that went awry. This was a huge political issue in Puerto Rico. They were especially grateful that I had gone down there, since I wasn't normally attached to Latino causes.

After we were released and traveled back up to New York, I moved on. I assumed that my Vieques ordeal was over. But several months later, in early May, I was attending a meeting in a hotel in Midtown when my cell phone rang. It was one of the guys I had met down in Puerto Rico.

"You know you go on trial tomorrow, right?" he said.

I shook my head. "No, that's just a court appearance. Just tell the lawyer I waive my appearance."

"No. The judge says trial."

"But I can't," I said. "It's three in the afternoon. How am I gonna get down there?"

"If you're not here, they're going to put out a federal warrant."

I was not pleased, but I knew a federal warrant was not something to mess with. I called the three other defendants and informed them of our dilemma. The next four hours were a blur, but we finally walked onto a seven thirty flight to San Juan, relieved and more than a bit annoyed. The next morning, we met briefly with our lawyers before we faced the judge. There were at least 100 other defendants there, all of them Vieques protesters. One by one, they started going before the federal judge, whose name was José Antonio Fusté. And every single one of them was getting jail time.

I looked at Ramirez; he looked back at me.

"We're going to jail today," I said.

He shook his head. "Oh, no, no, no. This is an appearance."

Again, I repeated, "We're going to jail."

When they called our case, the four of us stood up and went before Judge Fusté. One of our defense lawyers explained to the judge that three of us were elected officials and had to return to work. *Time* magazine had just told the world that I was thinking of running for president. We were busy guys. The hope was that the judge would give us a trial date for some point in the distant future.

"Fine. I understand all that," the judge responded. "Are you ready for trial?"

Before we knew what had hit us, the prosecutor was laying out his case against us. Of course, we were guilty—that's the whole point of civil disobedience. You want to get arrested, maybe even go to jail, to bring attention to your cause, to use the weight of public opinion to move the other side. After the prosecutor was finished, it was our turn to make our case. We had hired local counsel from Puerto Rico because we thought we were just making a court appearance. We weren't expecting an instant trial. Our lawyer stood up and stumbled through an ineffectual defense.

When he was done, Judge Fusté said, "OK, have a seat."

He turned to the four of us. "Be ready for sentencing. You're guilty."

Before our sentencing, we each had a chance to speak to the court.

"I don't come from Puerto Rico," I told the judge. "But I am one for standing up for something that is right. If Martin Luther King were alive, he would have come to Vieques to raise these issues. We believe that is his legacy. We owe a moral debt in the King tradition to stand up for children who can't stand up for themselves.

"This building will be closed next January in honor of Martin Luther King, who stood for civil rights," I continued. "Before you sentence me, I would like to wish you a happy King Day."

When it was time for sentencing, the judge called Ramirez's name. Ramirez stood. "Forty days," the judge said.

Next was Carrión. "Forty days."

Rivera. "Forty days."

Sharpton? "Oh, I see you've been arrested many times for civil rights," Judge Fusté said, looking down at my file. "You're a repeat offender. Ninety days."

Just like that. Three months in jail.

When I had left home the previous afternoon, I told my wife and two daughters, "I'm going to Puerto Rico for a hearing. I'll be right back."

Next thing I knew, I was in jail for the rest of the summer.

When we emerged from the courthouse, they had shackled not just our hands but also our feet. That was the federal way. My partners were clearly in a state of shock. But it was an important lesson for any activist preparing to participate in civil disobedience. You always have to be ready to go to jail. I don't care how important or indispensable you think you are. If there's a probability of arrest, then there's a possibility of jail. It's simply part of the activist job description.

I knew this would be a huge media story. The reason we had gone to Vieques in the first place was to bring attention to the harm the U.S. Navy was causing to the people of Puerto Rico and Vieques. So if the federal government was going to try to hit our burgeoning movement by imposing a harsh sentence on us, a sentence that might make the country take notice, then our job was to cooperate with the media in telling the story.

"Walk slow," I called out to the other guys, who were trying to hop quickly to the bus. "I want the whole world to see what they would do to us for saving some kids in Puerto Rico," I said.

And that was the picture that went out around the world— the four of us hopping in those stupid shackles. The images worked; the public was outraged by the entire spectacle.

When we were deposited in the federal facility, the New York senators, Chuck Schumer and Hillary Clinton, called to check on us. After two days, Schumer and Clinton arranged for us to be transferred to the federal jail in Brooklyn. They couldn't do anything to reduce our time, but they could have us moved to a more convenient location. If I was going to do three months in jail, I might as well do it in my hometown, smelling that sweet Brooklyn air!

When it was time for us to leave the facility in Puerto Rico, all the activists on that floor signed a bedsheet to thank me for doing so much for their cause. I still have that sheet, more than a decade later.

We had to keep those shackles on all the way to Kennedy Airport. When we landed, I looked out the window and saw twelve government cars on the tarmac. Twelve cars! Like they were bringing in John Gotti or something. They carted us to the Brooklyn House of Detention, where we would be doing our hard time.

In the meantime, a slew of lawyers, such as Harvard Law School professor Charles Ogletree, were running around to the appellate courts, trying to get our sentences reduced or thrown out. But I was resolved that we should do the time.

"Let me tell you something," I told my co-inmates. "They can go all the way to the Supreme Court. We are not getting out of here. We will do every day."

The federal authorities put us on a tier all by ourselves. They didn't want us in the general population. It quickly became clear that they couldn't let anything happen to us. That would be a public-relations disaster. So there we were, four men in a ward that was large enough for ninety. We could sleep in whatever cell we wanted, could watch a bunch of different TVs.

One of the most dramatic things I came up with to break the tedium was a fast. Nothing steals away the boredom like the growl of an empty stomach. A fast would continue to apply pressure on the authorities while keeping the public's eye on our cause. It was a classic political-prisoner tactic, used by everybody from Gandhi to Nelson Mandela and Martin Luther King Jr. After we started the fast, we would get a visit from the doctor twice a day, taking our blood, checking and double-checking that we weren't getting sick. They could not have us getting sick in their custody.

Whenever the doctor would come, I'd say, "Here comes Dracula to take my blood." That was our little joke.

I was getting lots of visits from my family. My wife came nearly every day. They let my daughters come in to see me twice. After my mother visited me, she went outside and talked to the media, one of the only times she ever talked to the press. They asked her if she had talked me into eating.

"No, he said he's not going to eat," she said. "All I can do is pray for him. He said he doesn't want to eat. I believe God is able."

After the forty days came and went, my partners in crime left me in that big chilly ward all by myself. Before they went home, they made me promise that I would eat at least one meal a day. They didn't want to leave; they were so wracked with guilt. They kept saying to me, "We're Latino, but you gotta do fifty days alone."

Once they were gone, there I was, just one man in this huge ward, alone for fifty days. Sometimes I'd have a visitor, but visiting hours ended at eight P.M. After that, it was just me and one lone corrections officer.

However, an amazing thing happened during those fifty days in that federal jail. In a sense, I had a fifty-day-long meeting with Al Sharpton. I had been on a treadmill all my life, always rushing from one tragedy or outrage to the next, always with a great sense of urgency, life-or-death stuff. But rarely had I taken the time to sit down and ask myself, *Where are you going? What is your ultimate purpose here?*

It dawned on me that I could take advantage of this rare opportunity for self-reflection. It was time for me to take a personal inventory and make some important decisions about my future.

As I look back on it, many of the amazing things that happened to me during the next decade of my life—syndicated radio show, national talk show, total reversal in how I was perceived by the public, sitting onstage at the Obama inauguration—were a direct result of those fifty days alone in jail. I guess I should take a minute to thank the venerable Judge Fusté down in Puerto Rico.

One of the things I decided was that I was going to devote myself to the National Action Network, make it bigger, more progressive, more national in scope.

I decided that I was going to focus on my health and my diet in a way I never had before. I began exercising every day and vowed to eat healthy foods. They were the first steps toward a change in lifestyle that resulted in my ultimately losing nearly 150 pounds—basically, I shed an entire person. (I wasn't able to keep off the weight I lost in Vieques, though. The real weight loss wouldn't come until a decade later.)

I did a lot of reading, devouring books by serious thinkers such as Paul Tillich, Arnold Toynbee, Reinhold Niebuhr, Nelson Mandela. It became clear to me that serious movements inevitably always must broaden. From the African National Congress in South Africa to Lech Walesa's Solidarity movement in Poland to the civil rights movement in the American South, in order to grow, each of these movements had to expand beyond its sectarian beginnings. You either grow and expand, or you die a quick death. Many of the civil rights organizations, such as CORE and even the SCLC to some degree, died out or were drastically streamlined because they didn't expand and build the next generation.

In every group, there are extremists who don't want to hear anything about expansion or growth. They will challenge you, accuse you of betraying the group by reaching out to others. It's such a common step in group dynamics that it's almost a cliché. This makes the development of a movement tougher, because you're going to take some shots from the people inside your own crowd. Malcolm X had to go through this, as did MLK and Mandela. You might be tempted to play to the cheap seats in your crowd, going after the easy targets, repeating the same campaigns, the same slogans, over and over. But you won't grow. The real loyalists, the ones who are truly committed to achieving a goal—rather than making themselves feel good or seeking vengeance—will understand the need for growth.

After reading about other movements, I became even more committed to establishing a strong and lasting bond with the Latino community. I saw it as the only way forward for black people in America.

I was fortunate that Vieques forced me to step off the treadmill and look inward. It was a time-out that I wasn't looking for, one that I never would have chosen on my own. But it was certainly a crucial process for me. I think most of us need to do that type of self-assessment from time to time, but we rarely get the time or opportunity to do it. If I hadn't been locked away in a Brooklyn prison, I'm sure I wouldn't have done it, either. So what started out for me as one of the low points of my career, with shackles and strip searches and long, lonely nights in an empty ward, in the end turned out to be one of the most important periods of my life. What I learned during those fifty days was how necessary it is for personal growth and transformation for every single one of us to take occasional time-outs to work on ourselves. It feels almost antithetical to the growth process—how can you grow and improve yourself by doing nothing? But I think many of us use the busy work as a distraction, a way to avoid asking ourselves the hard questions. It's like what happens in a troubled marriage when a baby comes along and takes the focus off the fraying marital bond; but then the baby starts growing up, needing less attention, and the couple turns back to each other, only to realize there's very little left to save in their marriage. If we can allow ourselves to step off the hamster wheel from time to time, maybe even go somewhere to get away from the craziness that swirls around us, I think it can be enormously beneficial. I got my little vacation right there in my hometown of Brooklyn, free of charge.

15

DEFINE YOURSELF—BEFORE OTHERS DO IT FOR YOU

One of the most valuable lessons James Brown taught me was the importance of defining yourself instead of letting others define you. Considering the incredible amount of nasty attacks and characterizations I've gotten in the media over the years, this became one of the most vital lessons I've ever learned.

James was born in the woods in South Carolina and raised in Augusta, Georgia. When he was three, his mother left. He never saw her again until he was starring at the Apollo Theater. When James was six, his father left him with his aunt, who ran a whorehouse in Augusta. Before James went to live with his aunt, his father would be gone all day, trying to find trees to tap for turpentine, leaving James alone in the woods for long periods of time. He said his best friends were the doodlebugs and insects. But this time allowed James to develop his own personality, one that was quite independent of what others thought of him.

One day, James said to me, "Reverend, there's one thing I always want you to promise me."

"What's that?" I said.

"Don't ever be one of the boys," he said. "Always define yourself. I learned in the woods that I had to depend on myself, make myself what I wanted to be. Don't mold yourself after somebody else."

In the end, I wanted to be able to go to my grave saying I had helped build a movement that made a difference. In order to do that, you have to build alliances, extend yourself, push the envelope. Move outside of your comfort zone. Otherwise, what's it all for?

If not for those months of reflection in 2001, I might not have been open to taking a path that would ultimately lead me to my own show on MSNBC. That wasn't something that was in the script of a civil rights leader. Yeah, Jesse Jackson had a show at one point, but being a TV talk-show host is not really in the activist handbook. If I had been listening over the years to the nasty ways in which I had been defined by others, if I had let the negativity of those *New York Post* cartoons seep into my soul, I probably would have been too afraid to put myself out there on a national television show, where my continued existence, my survival, would be determined by a national viewership of predominantly white Americans. I would have run away from such an opportunity, because I would have believed my press and accepted what others were saying.

I work eighteen hours a day now, because I'm purpose-driven. I'm trying to make a difference, on my own terms. I wake up at four or five most mornings, hopping onto a plane to somewhere, to the next crisis, pushed by the thought in the back of my mind: *What can I do today to make a difference?*

I think people sense that drive and purpose in me, which is why they don't begrudge me the first-class flights and the fancy hotels to which I now have access. They know I've earned it. People know that I bear the marks of the struggles on my body. I'm fifty-eight years old, as of this writing. I've been stabbed. I've spent months in jail. I've gone through all kinds of controversies over the years. There's not much left you can do to me, except kill me.

Even when I was marching in the early days with the pressed hair, the jogging suits, and the medallions—all objects that certainly added to the scornful characterizations of me, items that made me an easy caricature—I wasn't too worried about how others would perceive me. If I had been afraid of the ways I would be portrayed in the media, I would not have chosen that particular style as my introduction to the world. But I was all about the movement, the message. I didn't care what they wrote, how they tried to ridicule me, because in my mind, I had a clear idea of what I was trying to accomplish. I knew what Al Sharpton stood for.

There aren't many bad days for me, because I can always think of something worse. Having a turbulent flight to Cleveland in first class isn't a bad day for me, not with everything I've endured. When you live your life like that, on the edge, you don't ever let yourself get too high or too low, too excited or too depressed, 'cause you've seen it all.

Too many of us spend our lives as spectators, watching other people, rather than trying to do things ourselves, make our own contributions. Maybe one of the reasons is that it's not easy to step out there by yourself, especially if you've been spending too many of your days letting others define you. But as I tell the young folks all the time in the National Action Network, if it's easy, it ain't worth having. I talk about my ninety days in jail, but can you imagine Nelson Mandela sitting there for twenty-seven years? And he never had any idea whether he'd ever get out until the very end. He certainly never dreamed he'd be president of the country; I'm sure in his mind, that was never in the realm of possibility. But at some point, he defined for himself who he was—he'd rather be incarcerated than be free and not fight for liberation.

When I was protesting in Howard Beach or Bensonhurst or Vieques, I didn't say, "I want to do this so that one day, I'll have access to the president of the United States and go to the White House and the inauguration and have my own MSNBC show and have social stature." I did it all because I believed in what I was doing. Those other things were all rewards, but they weren't the reason.

16

DON'T BE AFRAID TO BE BIG

I only saw Martin Luther King a couple of times, because I was just thirteen when he was killed, but I did have the good fortune of getting to know Coretta Scott King very well. I had organized a big march in Washington with her son Martin III, to try to push President Bill Clinton into signing an executive order against racial profiling. The year was 2000. Martin III was president of the SCLC, and I had just expanded NAN to a national organization. Coretta was going to introduce us at the march, and I told her that we thought we might be getting as many as 100,000 people in attendance.

She said, "Al, always remember, the difference between Martin and a lot of other guys was he was big enough to be big. You can't be big and small at the same time. If you think small and parochial and get caught up in nonsense and mess and jealousy and envy, you will never grow to be the leader you can be. You gotta be big enough to do big things."

Those words have resonated with me precisely because I've seen so many great leaders, so many talented people, violate them, getting caught up in small, petty nonsense, drowning in those shallow waters. In activism, in progressive movements, even in the church, people get shrunk down and are trapped in smallness, like a fly wriggling on flypaper. Their talents are bigger than their character allows them to be. When they perceive a threat, they want to hold on to everything, protect their domain, lash out. But if it's great, if it's food for the soul, you're supposed to want to share it. In the religious community, you get a lot of small-mindedness and insecurity masquerading as theology—holding back others, opposing the rights of others, because you are trying to hold on to what you've got.

I once got into an argument with a black activist group that wanted to bar whites from its rallies. I said, "No, I'm not going to do that." But they were adamant. I told them, "Anything I say, anybody can hear. Why should I be insecure about white people hearing it?"

They wanted to have their own private, blacks-only meetings, but it didn't even make sense—they sold DVDs of their speeches. They were holding on to this secretive, clandestine view of their movement, and they were afraid to be big and bold enough to let everybody hear it.

Coretta's words have stayed with me over the years and have driven me. You need some greater purpose when you're standing there in the morgue alongside a mother who has been brought to identify her dead child—something I've had to do probably thirty or forty times. Trying to comfort her through her wails, I want to be able to tell her about the larger purpose of her pain, how I will fight to make sure her child didn't die in vain.

With Coretta's words ringing in my mind, I've seen some big things. I stood in the square in Johannesburg the night they brought down that apartheid flag and raised the flag of the ANC, bloodlessly turning the world's most racist regime into a democracy. I was there as an election observer with Wyatt Tee Walker and Danny Glover and others, witnessing Nelson Mandela become the president of South Africa.

I was there when Barack Obama put his hand on the Bible and became the forty-fourth president of the United States.

I've seen big things. I know what we can do, as a movement, as a people, as a country. We have to develop the skin to take the little hits and keep the big picture in mind. We can't be afraid to be big.

17

BE OPEN TO UNLIKELY ALLIES

The first time I laid my eyes on Barack Obama was in 2003, at Chicago's annual Bud Billiken Parade, which the African-American community in Chicago has been holding on the South Side on the second Saturday in August since 1929. I was serving as one of the grand marshals that year, and Obama was a state senator at the time. We acknowledged each other in passing, but we didn't really talk. His name stood out to me because it was so unusual and because he had sponsored legislation against racial profiling in the Illinois state legislature. NAN had been monitoring efforts across the country to combat racial profiling after Johnnie Cochran and I fought the rampant use of racial profiling by state troopers on the New Jersey Turnpike.

The first time we really talked was at the 2004 Democratic National Convention in Boston. We were both scheduled to speak at the Black Democratic Caucus, one of the many separate meetings that are held that week among various constituencies of the Democratic Party. I had run for president that year, so I had a bit of influence at the convention, where we were going to be nominating Massachusetts Sen. John Kerry as the Democratic candidate, with North Carolina Sen. John Edwards as his running mate. Dr. Charles Ogletree, the distinguished African-American professor at nearby Harvard Law School, brought Obama over to me. Ogletree was close to both of us, because he had mentored both Barack and Michelle Obama at the law school, and he was on my campaign committee and had done a lot of fund-raising for me. Obama had already spoken to the group and was preparing to leave as I was arriving to give my speech.

"You guys should know each other," Ogletree said. "You're not that far apart in age, from the same generation. Barack was one of my students at Harvard."

"Yeah, I know who he is," I said. "I wish you well in your election in Illinois."

He was running for the U.S. Senate in Illinois against black Republican Alan Keyes.

"Of course, I know who you are," he said to me. Then he started to tell me about his keynote address later that night at the Democratic National Convention. "I'm trying to do something to set a tone of unity in the country. I don't exactly do what you do, but we're both trying to make a better country."

As he continued explaining to me his broader approach, I cut him off. "You do what you have to do tonight—plus, you gotta get elected," I said, smiling. "I'm going to take care of the brothers and sisters tomorrow night when I speak."

He kind of looked at me closely for a second, and then he laughed. So from the very first moment we started conversing, we had established a template of straightforward honesty, acknowledging that we were not the same, we didn't have the same approach to our politics and activism, but we had broadly the same goals.

That night, I sat in one of the boxes and listened to Obama do his thing, rousing the crowd by talking about how unlikely it was for him to be standing on that stage. "In no other country on earth is my story even possible," he said. It was a well-constructed, memorable speech that put him on the political map, establishing him as a rising star. While I thought the speech was excellent, it was a bit mainstream for me. But I said to myself, *This guy is exciting*.

The next night, I took to the podium and went for the gusto. I talked about how we weren't living up to the "promise of America" under President George W. Bush. I even mentioned Barack Obama as I talked about a new generation of young leaders who may come from humble backgrounds but who have integrity and family values. Bush had suggested that the black community was being taken for granted by the Democratic Party, so I explained why we had hitched our fate to the Democrats and told him that our vote could not be bargained away or given away.

"Mr. President, the reason we are fighting so hard, the reason we took Florida so seriously, is our right to vote wasn't gained because of our age," I said as the crowd roared. "Our vote was soaked in the blood of martyrs, soaked in the blood of Goodman, Chaney, and Schwerner, soaked in the blood of four little girls in Birmingham. This vote is sacred to us."

A couple of years later, in 2006, I started hearing rumblings about whether Obama, who had destroyed Keyes in the 2004 Senate election by one of the largest margins in Senate history, was going to run for president in 2008. Since I had been a candidate in 2004 and had begun to be seen as a national black leader with some clout, I started hearing from all the candidates who were running—New Mexico Gov. Bill Richardson, Delaware Sen. Joe Biden, North Carolina Sen. John Edwards. And of course, New York Sen. Hillary Clinton. As far as I could tell, everyone assumed I would be supporting Clinton—after all, she was the senator from my state, she had been a frequent presence at NAN's annual conventions, and she had even spoken at our King Day celebration at the House of Justice in Harlem. So I suppose from the outside it looked like a no-brainer. But then there was the matter of her husband. I had a complicated relationship with the former president. I supported him and called a march for him when he was being impeached, but I also felt that he fell short on a number of issues, such as racial profiling and police brutality. I was bitterly opposed to his welfare reform bill and his omnibus crime bill, both of which I felt would do considerable harm to poor people and people of color. So my feelings about him were somewhat mixed.

My first meeting with President Clinton was memorable.

He was midway through his first term and was speaking at the 1995 Congressional Black Caucus dinner. I was there with Reverend Jackson.

"Let's go to the rope when the president finishes speaking," Jesse said, leaning over to me during his speech. "I haven't been able to get a meeting with him. We need to talk to him about building all these jails and no jobs."

So we went over to the rope at the conclusion of the speech to see if we could get a word with Clinton. He made his way down the rope line, squeezing hands and slapping backs, as he does so well. When he got to us, Jesse said, "I've been trying to get a meeting with you. I think—"

The president cut him off halfway through his sentence. "Well, come on over to the residence tonight," he said. "I'll have Harold Ickes bring you in. And bring Al with you." Ickes was Clinton's deputy chief of staff and had worked on Jesse's presidential campaign a decade earlier.

With head-spinning alacrity, just a few hours later, I was sitting in the Treaty Room in the residence of the White House, waiting for the president, along with Reverend Jesse Jackson, Jesse Jackson, Jr., who was running for Congress for the first time, and Jesse Jr.'s wife, Sandi. Clinton came into the room, wearing blue jeans and a big smile. Jesse and I began laying out our case to him on why the country needed more jobs programs, not jails, and why we were opposed to some of his triangulation policies. We were engaged in an energetic back-and-forth dialogue, with Ickes sitting in, when Clinton popped up and said, "Y'all want some cherry pie?"

So as we sat there waiting, the president of the United States went to get us cherry pie. While he was gone, Jesse teased me: "I'm going to tell the fellas in Harlem that you sold out for some cherry pie."

We all laughed. Soon after, Clinton came back and asked Jesse Jr. and me, "Y'all ever seen the Lincoln Bedroom?"

We shook our heads. I had been to the White House a couple of times—the first time with James Brown during the Reagan administration—but I had never been in the residence. So we followed the president to the Lincoln Bedroom, and then he brought us to another room, where we looked in awe at the Emancipation Proclamation.

When we sat down again, Reverend Jackson told Clinton and Ickes that Jesse Jr. was running for Congress and could really use their help. They agreed to help him, which was a promise on which they did follow through. Then Clinton had a request of us. By now it was close to one A.M.

"This Million Man March that's happening next month— what do you think I should do?" he asked. "Some people are saying we should attack Minister Farrakhan."

I decided to answer that one. "Let me tell you something. Minister Farrakhan may do or say things that a lot of people don't agree with. I don't even agree with everything he's said and done. And I know he doesn't agree with everything I've said and done. But like Dr. King, he's galvanized something that's important. I don't think you should attack him."

Jesse suggested that Clinton let the march proceed and perhaps find something else to do that day. It turned out that on the day of the march, Clinton did travel out of town, to the University of Texas, and delivered one of his most sweeping speeches on race, asking Americans to "clean our house of racism." However, in the speech, he did take a swipe at Louis Farrakhan and the march, saying, "One million men do not make right one man's message of malice and division."

So while Clinton and I had been allies, it wasn't all milk and honey.

In early 2007, I decided I needed to know what each of the candidates for president stood for and what they were thinking about how to solve the nation's problems. So I toured Washington and met with each of them, which was easy, since almost all of them were in the Senate. Obama was the last meeting, the end of my gauntlet of senators. When I walked into his office, I was struck by the poignancy of the huge picture of Supreme Court Justice Thurgood Marshall that he had on his wall. I thought it fit, because that was the tradition that had birthed him, the former law school professor—the world of jurisprudence, where Marshall clearly had been a pioneer.

As we talked, I liked Obama's thinking, his approach to problem solving, but I wasn't sure if he was strong enough on black issues, which was a common criticism he was hearing at the time in the black community. At the same time, I was getting the red-carpet treatment from the Clintons—Bill was speaking at the NAN convention, Hillary at the NAN women's luncheon. Actually, we had every one of the Democratic candidates speak at the NAN convention that year. I was quite the popular guy, with the suitors lined up to punch my dance card. But I was not about to let it go to my head; I knew it was just part of the political game, the methodical courting of each constituent group that you must do when you run for president, like an accountant tallying numbers in a ledger.

At that point, I still hadn't made up my mind which candidate I would support. I was leaning toward Hillary, but I kind of liked Obama. I got a call one day from Charlie King, who was the acting executive director of NAN at the time and who was a longtime Democratic Party operative in New York State. King told me that President Clinton was flying home to Chappaqua and wanted to meet with me at the house there. I traveled up to Chappaqua and met with the former president for about an hour. He persuasively laid out all the reasons I should go with his wife. It was a convincing presentation, and I was almost there, right on the verge of giving Hillary the nod. But on the drive back to Manhattan, one of my associates who was in the car with me managed to say something that changed my perspective a bit. First, he asked me, "Have you decided what you're going to do—Clinton or Obama?"

"I don't know," I answered truthfully. "I'm kind of going back and forth on it."

Obama had also been laying on the charm. He had come up to New York and asked if he could take me out to dinner. He came by the House of Justice in Harlem, already accompanied by the Secret Service, and scooped me up. We went to Sylvia's Restaurant in Harlem, with the national media in tow and making a big deal about him having soul food in Harlem.

"I remember when all the black leaders went against you in '04," my associate reminded me. "I guess it didn't hurt them."

That comment stayed with me for a minute. I went up into the Grand Havana Room, a private club where I like to unwind and smoke cigars several evenings a week, and I thought some more about it, how the New York leadership didn't feel the need to rally around me when I ran; this idea of regional loyalties didn't seem to apply for me. My decision had been made. I went into a private area of the club, and I called Obama.

"I met today with President Clinton," I told him.

"Yeah, yeah, I know you have to work on policy with her," he said. "All I ask is, if you can't support me, try not to hurt me."

"Nah, I think I'm going to support you."

"Huh?" he said, clearly shocked. "I never asked you to do that."

"No, you didn't," I said. "In my own way, I'm going to go out there and support you. I don't even know if you can win. Probably, tonight, I *don't* think you can win. But it won't be because I was in the way. I won't do to you what a lot of folks did to me."

Clearly, he was very thankful—and surprised.

A few weeks passed, and I got a call from Obama. They were having a black forum focusing on urban affairs in Iowa, the location of the first Democratic primary/caucus. They had asked me to be the keynote speaker. Obama said he had to go because all the other candidates were going. He wanted to know how we could pull it off without bumping heads, because our approaches to the black agenda would be different and

181

might even at times be in conflict. He didn't want to sound as if he was in opposition to anything I might say, but at the same time, he didn't want to hurt his campaign.

"How do we do this?" he asked me.

"Let me think about it and get back to you," I said.

I later found out there had been debate among his staff about how to handle Iowa and Sharpton. He had decided to call me directly, rather than having a surrogate call me, which I appreciated. After a couple of days of deliberation, I called him back on his cell phone.

"I thought about how we can do this," I said.

"OK, what do you think we should do?" he asked.

"I'm not going," I said.

"What do you mean, you're not going? I didn't ask you not to go."

"There's no way I can go and not say things that they would try to use against you, because I'm going to be Al Sharpton. But if I don't go, there won't be any potential conflict—and they might not even have it. So I'm not going."

"Wow," he said. "You know, it's rare to meet people who can see things are bigger than them."

"Hey, all of us in public life got ego," I said. "But all of us should remember there are things bigger than us. So I'm out."

After we called the folks in Iowa to tell them I would be bowing out of the keynote, they did eventually cancel it. I think that whole exchange revealed to each of us important things about the other. Obama saw that I had a self-awareness and humility that allowed me to take myself out of the picture for the greater good, which was his election. And I was surprised and impressed that he valued my counsel and help enough to call me on the phone himself. After that, we started communicating on a fairly regular basis. I also talked directly to Valerie Jarrett, a very good friend of the Obamas from Chicago who was a close adviser of his. Let me just say that in the more than four decades I've been in public life, I don't think I've met anyone who had more integrity in their dealings with me than Valerie Jarrett. She never told me she was going to do something that she didn't do. And if she didn't agree with me about something or it was something they weren't going to do, she would tell me that, too. Her degree of sincerity and truthfulness is truly rare in public life. When I've heard people in the African-American community question the president's closeness to the black community, whether he got a sense of what was happening with us or the difficulties we were having, I never doubted for a second that he got this kind of crucial intelligence, because I knew Valerie was at his side. I have found that not only does she have a great deal of influence, but she also has enormous integrity. When I relay issues or concerns to her, she doesn't jump because we said jump. With her, you have a strong woman who makes her own decisions, because she knows our community as well as we do.

As the campaign was just starting to heat up, the Rev. Jeremiah Wright story broke, with the media condemning Obama for being a member for twenty years of Trinity United Church of Christ in Chicago and playing in a seemingly endless loop the footage of a tiny portion of a Wright sermon during which he proclaims, "God damn America!" I talked about Wright with Obama and with Valerie, and I knew he was trying his best to have that story go away as quickly as possible. I went on different talk shows to defend his position. It was a dilemma for him because he wanted to be respectful of his pastor, but he had to come forward and denounce some of what the reverend said while pointing out that Wright's words were being distorted. So he had about three different positions he was trying to take at the same time, which is a nearly impossible predicament for a politician to maneuver out of—and which will leave a bad taste in a lot of people's mouths.

What was especially upsetting for me was the idea that Wright was being attacked as some type of racial arsonist when the tenor of his words was not racial at all. He was questioning America; what was racial about it? To say "God damn America" might be interpreted as disrespectful, but where is it racial? The whole ordeal created problems for me internally, because not only did I know Reverend Wright, but his daughter Jeri was head of the NAN chapter in Chicago. So here I was supporting Obama by saying that he did all he could to respect his pastor but that some of Wright's comments were extreme, and I was going against my own chapter leader. As you could expect, the conflict temporarily tore up our Chicago chapter. And I had a lot of ministers taking Wright's side and asking me how I could support Obama and say he was doing the right thing when he was being critical of Wright. That was the first round of friction that I took for my support of Obama.

With my late mother
Ada Sharpton, 2001.

In the Sudan, 2001.

Meeting with Israeli Foreign
Minister Shimon Peres in
Tel Aviv, Israel, 2001.

With Rabbi Marc
Schneier, Henry
Kissinger and
Rabbi Boteach,
2001.

Receiving a gift from Yasser Arafat at his headquarters in Palestine, 2001.

Handcuffed and jailed in
Vieques, Puerto Rico, 2001.

Working at my desk with
Michael Jackson, 2002.

(left) Mobbed at the Democratic National Convention at New York University, 2002.

(middle) At the 2004 Democratic Presidential Candidate Debate with (left to right) Joe Lieberman, John Edwards, Howard Dean, and Bob Graham.

With Bill Clinton and Jesse Jackson at John Johnson's funeral in Chicago, 2005.

Standing by the body of James Brown on stage at the Apollo, 2006.

Leading the body of James Brown from the National Action Network head-quarters in Harlem to the Apollo, 2006.

Eating with presidential candidate Barack Obama at Sylvia's restaurant in Harlem, late 2007.

Former NYC Mayor Dinkins and U.S. Senator Hillary Clinton conferring in my office, April 2007.

Meeting with President Bush at a Philadelphia school, January 2009.

Leading the Anti-Stop and Frisk March, 2012.

Leading the National Action Network's 2012 Anti-Voter ID Law March from Selma to Montgomery.

Speaking at a Justice for Trayvon Rally in Florida on
March 31, 2012.

Occupy the Corner, a National Action Network anti-violence drive, at
midnight in 2012.

Greeting Jay-Z and Beyoncé on the platform at the second inauguration for President Obama. Beyoncé later sang the national anthem.

Opening my show PoliticsNation on MSNBC. *(used with the permission of MSNBC)*

I was trying to get my colleagues to see the bigger picture. The man was running for president, with a very legitimate chance to win. Wright was coming out of a prophetic tradition of black pastors—as I do—who are charged to speak truth to power and lead our people out of oppression. These are two very different agendas that are not always going to be heading in the same direction.

I think the Wright saga demonstrated to the then-senator that we both had different but crucial roles to play and, perhaps more important, that we could trust each other.

After Wright, we stepped into another controversy that managed to hit me even closer to home than the Wright stuff. During a television interview on Fox News, Reverend Jackson, not realizing that his mic was on, said under his breath that Obama was "talking down to black people" with his Father's Day comments, when Obama had said black men must stand up and do a better job of taking responsibility for their kids.

"I wanna cut his nuts off," Jackson added.

I went on Anderson Cooper's show on CNN that night and defended Obama again. I said I loved Reverend Jackson, that he had mentored me and I had learned a great deal from him, but I didn't agree with him. I said for a man to stand up on Father's Day and talk about how black men must be responsible for their kids is not talking down to us. For us to act as if being irresponsible is just a black thing is talking down to us. I also said that Jesse had made one mistake with an off-the-cuff remark, but let's not forget his forty years of

service. As I left CNN after doing Cooper's show and got back into the car to go to Fox to do Sean Hannity's show, I talked to Reverend Jackson. Let's just say he was less than happy with my position. After we hung up, I got a call from a friend at Fox who was a producer. I thought he was getting worried about my arrival. I told him I was on my way.

"Before you get out there too far in defending Jesse, you should know we have not released the whole tape," he said.

"What are you talking about?"

"Jesse also used the *n*-word," he said. "You know that word that y'all said we should bury?"

"He did what?" I said, making him repeat it. I felt a sinking feeling in my stomach. Jesse had used the *n*-word in reference to Obama? That was an entirely different matter.

I hung up and immediately called Jesse back. "You used the *n*-word?" I asked him when he picked up.

"Nah, I didn't use the *n*-word," he said. "I don't believe that."

Two weeks later, Fox released the full video, which confirmed that Reverend Jackson did, in fact, use the *n*-word. The incident certainly didn't help Reverend Jackson's relationship with the Obama camp.

Senator Obama saw that not only did I understand what he strategically had to do for his candidacy, but I was also fighting with people I had decades of history with, on his behalf. By the time they got to the last primaries, I had upset much of the civil rights community, many of the black preachers, and pretty much all of the politicians in New York State for going against Hillary. To my surprise, Obama won. So in hindsight,

I looked brilliant, but I had no idea when I decided to support him that he would win the nomination.

That 2008 election campaign showed me how crucial it is to keep the big picture in your sights, even when there's a hellish storm swirling all around you. It is a lesson whose importance the Obama team demonstrated on an almost daily basis during the campaign, a lesson I would think a man on the verge of becoming the first black president would need to repeat to himself over and over as race and politics slammed together and led people to say some crazy stuff about him and his wife.

One day in the midst of the summer, as the Democrats were gearing up for the convention in Denver, I got a call on my cell phone as I was riding through the Holland Tunnel for a speaking engagement in New Jersey. I looked down and saw that it was Senator Obama, who was supposed to be on a family vacation in Hawaii.

"How are you doing back there?" he said.

"I'm doing fine," I answered. "I thought you weren't calling people during your vacation?"

"Al, to tell you the truth, I talked to the president of Russia today, and I talked to you. Those are my business calls."

"Wow, I'm honored," I said.

He laughed. "The day I'm accepting the nomination is the anniversary of Dr. King's March on Washington and the 'I Have a Dream' speech," he said. "I'm going to have the Democratic Party host an official breakfast that morning. I want to have Martin III, Bernice, and you as the speakers. And I just want you to know I appreciate you." I thanked him and hung up the phone. He followed through on that breakfast, with all the civil rights guys there, with Martin III and me doing the keynote. I brought my daughters with me, too.

Later that night, before we headed to the stadium to watch a black man receive the Democratic Party nomination for president, I got into a car with my daughters to go to the convention center to do my radio show. My cell phone rang. It was Obama.

"Thank you for the words you said this morning," he said. "Valerie called and told me what you said."

"It's a great day," I said to him. "I hope you win the election, but just winning the nomination is a great thing. I brought my daughters here with me to see it."

"Your daughters are with you?" he said. "Let me speak to them."

So I handed them the phone, and he talked to Dominique and then Ashley. It was the thrill of their lives, to talk to Barack Obama on the day he was nominated.

After the rigors of that campaign and the frequent questions I got from the civil rights community and the black church community, I was even more convinced of the need to stick to your principles when you're being threatened and attacked. As we all watched Senator Obama run a brilliant campaign against John McCain and become President Obama, I could breathe a little easier. It had all been worth it. My relationship with Barack Obama has taught me an important lesson about being open to unlikely alliances and unexpected friendships.

With his Ivy League background and mainstream approach, he would seem an unnatural fit for the fiery preacher and civil rights leader from the Brooklyn streets. But when we remained open to the possibilities of an alliance, we discovered that, in fact, we retained an easy understanding and respect for each other. With our very different approaches, we usually wound up in the same place, fighting the same battles.

18

DON'T BE AFRAID TO ASK FOR
WHAT YOU WANT

A few months after Obama's inauguration in January 2009, I asked Valerie Jarrett if we could have a meeting at the White House to discuss inequality in education and the huge achievement gap between black students and white students. I had convinced former House Speaker Newt Gingrich, about as visible and conservative a Republican as you could find, to come to the meeting with me, because I wanted to show that it was a societal problem with bipartisan support

The meeting took place with Gingrich; New York Mayor Michael Bloomberg, a Republican who had endorsed Obama; and me. Los Angeles Mayor Antonio Villaraigosa was supposed to come, but at the last minute, he had to stay in L.A. because of union negotiations. When the president addressed the NAACP at the 100th anniversary celebration, he told the story about sitting in the Oval Office, looking at me and then at

Gingrich, and not believing that we were sitting there in his office together.

Gingrich and I had developed a respectful relationship over the years, based on our common ground of major education reform to address inequalities, which we both felt was a civil rights issue. He even addressed the NAN convention one year. Of course, there's a lot in his educational platform that I don't agree with, such as vouchers and diverting money and space away from the public schools for a bunch of experimental charter schools that reach just a tiny percentage of the population.

At the White House meeting, Arne Duncan, the president's education secretary, came up with the idea of Gingrich and me going out together on a national tour to bring attention to the need for education reform. Gingrich and I, along with Duncan, went to five cities, culminating in an appearance on *Meet the Press*, where we talked about education as a civil rights issue—because, ultimately, if you do not give equal educational preparation to Americans, you're never going to have an equal society.

The education tour was a revealing illustration of how Obama seems to view me in a different way from his predecessors. It's amusing that I've gotten attacked for my access to Obama, because I spent considerable time in the White House when Clinton and Bush were president. But I guess, in Bush's case, when a conservative Republican does it, it's reaching out; when a Democratic black president does it, it's called pandering. But the difference with Obama was that he would invite me to meetings about issues that weren't directly related to race.

So I'd be at a White House meeting with white progressive leaders or a meeting on immigration where I'd be sitting next to Mayor Bloomberg and California Gov. Arnold Schwarzenegger. Obama sees black leadership as part of American leadership, not as a separate entity over in the corner that is preoccupied with race. He's a worldly man with a huge range of issues that he's concerned about; he recognizes that other black leaders could be the same. Also, he knows that if he's going to have a successful initiative, he needs everybody working together. If he has to get Elena Kagan confirmed for the Supreme Court, he's going to need labor, he's going to need civil rights, he's going to need the support of a wide swath of constituencies. So instead of meeting with us separately, Obama will bring all of us to the White House together.

Whenever I'm around Obama, I always come away with the feeling that this is a serious, cerebral, very deliberate sort of guy. Even during light moments, there's a heaviness about him. I've been around him at social events that are supposed to be fun, such as the White House Super Bowl party, but that feeling never really goes away. He always seems to be looking at the bigger picture, a step or two beyond everybody else. He doesn't appear to have any hint of pettiness about him. Even with presidents, you can sometimes see an emotional reaction to things, a desire to get back at somebody for a perceived slight. But there's none of that with Obama. He really wants to be a great president, a transformative president. It's not nearly enough for him to be the first black president or a two-term president. He is shooting for heights that are much loftier, up there with Abraham Lincoln and Franklin Roosevelt. Unlike some politicians I've known who were happy to be the first black mayor of a city and had no vision beyond that, or the first black CEO of a major corporation but with no real goal greater than that, Obama from the first day was there to make a difference in the lives of all Americans. He was committed to big ideas, such as health-care reform, finance reform, tax reform.

I heard a scholar criticize him by saying he doesn't understand the legacy of Dr. King and Ella Baker. When I heard that, I thought, *He's not trying to be Dr. King and Ella Baker. He's trying to be John Kennedy and Lyndon Johnson.* Civil rights leaders like me, we're trying to be Dr. King and Ella Baker. Once you understand that distinction, you have a much clearer picture of Barack Obama and his relationship to the black community. He wasn't trying to be Booker T. Washington; he was trying to be George Washington. When I hear people in the black community take umbrage at the notion that he's not the president of black America but the president of all America, I feel insulted, because it feels to me as if we're saying that this black man should be loyal just to us, rather than giving him space to run the world. I think we limit his ability to soar when we try to reduce him to something we're used to, something we are better able to grasp.

As a civil rights leader in the age of Obama, I had to wrestle with a question that my predecessors never had to face: how to deal with a black head of state. Dr. King didn't have that challenge. The young Jesse Jackson didn't have that challenge.

So for me, there was no model to study. I have always been one to look back and get some counsel from those who came before, by reading everything they wrote and what others said about them. From my earliest years, this has always been my way, to immerse myself in the books to gain greater understanding. But there was nothing I could read to prepare me for this. What do you do with a black head of state who has the sentiment and the heart of the people you're serving, yet you still need to hold him accountable? This is all new ground. It may be fifty years before scholars will be able to analyze whether we did it right or wrong, because right now, there's really nothing to gauge it against. How do you hold him accountable without undermining him at the same time? It's a daily dilemma—issue by issue, bill by bill. Do you go in and challenge him in the Oval Office, maybe as he sits behind that big desk, surrounded by the breathtaking symbols of American history and power? Do you gather your forces and march on him outside the White House, luring the national media to try to embarrass him into action?

Interestingly, I think he has the same dilemma. How does he deal with black leadership as a black president? Not showing preference but at the same time showing deference? These are all questions that are being worked out by Obama on a daily basis. If he calls me too often, does he then render me less effective and less useful to him? But if he doesn't call any of us, will he then be accused of detaching himself from the black community?

I should add that you can't talk about the grace and

seriousness of Obama without talking about the tremendous talents that his wife, Michelle, brings to the table. I think her symbol and her substance—in terms of issues such as her focus on America's health and the well-being of military families—have been very effective, but her personal charisma is overwhelming. When you are with her, you feel a genuine concern and love for people. One of the highlights of my life was going to the White House in 2011 for the Super Bowl party. I brought my older daughter, Dominique, with me; Ashley was away at college. It was in the East Room of the White House, where we walked in and saw about thirty tables, each with four chairs, and two very large TV screens. After we had arrived, the president came in with the first lady, the girls, and Michelle's mother, Marian Robinson. Everyone was dressed down, in sweaters and slacks. As I sat there talking to my daughter—we were the only ones at our table—I suddenly felt these arms slide around my neck. I looked up, and it was the first lady. She hugged me and then sat down at our table. She began talking to my daughter, going in like a big sister or an auntie. "What are your plans? What are your goals in life? Don't ever think you can't do whatever you want to do. People are not smarter than you." It was basic but challenging, hard stuff. This was not the superficial conversation you might expect in the situation. I could see that she was really getting to my daughter; Dominique was soaking it up. It was stuff I would say to her, but she would expect me to say it. But here was the first lady of the United States, sitting in the White House, lecturing her that she needed to be serious about her life, that she couldn't just rest on her last name, that she had to go out there and make her own mark. While I was sitting there listening, I looked over Dominique's head and saw a portrait of George Washington gazing out over the room. I chuckled to myself. Did George ever imagine there would be a black first lady in the White House telling the daughter of a black civil rights leader to focus on her life? It just showed me how far we had come, sitting there in that big house that slaves had built.

While I was soaking in the moment, the president walked over and started laughing. "For the last twenty minutes, I saw something I never thought I'd see," he said. "All I saw was Al Sharpton's head going up and down, not saying a word, not getting a word in edgewise. Now you know how I feel when I go to the residence at night." We all laughed. It's a day I'll never forget. I'm sure Dominique won't, either.

Michelle Obama is very direct, very blunt, but loving at the same time. I've been very impressed with her. Together, the two of them have it all—he's more studious and deliberate, she's more outgoing. And their affection for each other is real. What you see of them publicly is also how they are privately. I don't think there's any pretense to their bond and their love. The pressures on their relationship have to be enormous, but they seem to handle them well. They are exemplary role models for the entire country on how to sustain a strong marriage in the midst of crazy stress. I don't know if Michelle Obama will ever run for office, but if she did, she'd be a hell of an officeholder. She's extremely smart, and she has an instinctive feel for people. She'd certainly get my support.

After Obama's reelection, I got together with other black

leaders such as Ben Jealous of the NAACP and Marc Morial of the National Urban League to craft a black agenda to bring to the president. I think it's something that we should have done earlier, during his first term. Obama got attacked by a lot of black activists and the black academic community, who felt he wasn't doing enough for the black community. While I had my disagreements with the administration—I felt we should have withdrawn immediately from Afghanistan; I'm opposed to our use of drones; I want them to close Guantanamo Bay—I didn't buy the strategy of the black opposition. If you have a list of things you think he should be doing, why not write them down and present your list to him? At least, that way, there will be something by which you can judge his actions on your behalf. Because otherwise, as happened during his first term, he will take a series of actions, such as health-care reform or auto-industry rescue, and he will claim they were to the benefit of your community. But then you respond that they weren't the *right* actions, or they weren't the actions you wanted him to take. With a specific agenda, at least everyone's on the same page.

What I kept hearing was: He did stuff for Latinos, such as protections for the children of some undocumented immigrants; he did stuff for gays, such as stopping "Don't Ask, Don't Tell" and supporting same-sex marriage; he did stuff for women, such as the Lilly Ledbetter Fair Pay Act, which helps women seek equal pay. But my response was, yeah, and the women's groups brought him Lilly Ledbetter, gay groups fought for same-sex marriage, Latino groups brought him the DREAM Act and immigration reform, and I even led a march with them in Arizona. He didn't sit down on his own and just pull this stuff from his imagination. They all brought these issues to him. So what the black activists are saying is, because he's black, they want him to write the black agenda and bring it to himself? And then, if I meet with him and talk about a black agenda, I'm too close, and I'm a sellout? It sounds like a catch-22 to me.

I think a lot of the criticism was coming from a place of insecurity, almost like the nervous high school kid who likes the pretty girl but isn't sure if he's good enough for her, so instead of asking her out, he's going to wait for her to call him to prove she really likes him. And then he's devastated when she never calls; never mind the fact that she may never have been aware that he wanted her to call. At times, it also felt as if many in the black community didn't understand that Obama was really the president. The honest-to-goodness leader of the free world. Some of us had a hard time wrapping our heads around that. When he came to speak at the NAN convention, some of my staff were shocked that basically the entire block had to be shut down, cordoned off. I was thinking, *Yes, that's what they do to protect the president! Every president.* Sometimes the tone of the Obama criticisms felt as if critics were saying, "He didn't come by my fish fry, so I'm going to attack him." And then they started attacking me: Sharpton can't be that close to the president and still be a civil rights leader. Really? Andrew Young, a civil rights leader, became United Nations ambassador for Jimmy Carter. But that was all right. Jesse Jackson was envoy to Africa for Bill Clinton. But that was all right. I don't have a job or an appointment with

Barack Obama; I just have access to him. So when did everyone have a meeting and change the rules? I didn't get the memo. And besides, leaders far greater than me, such as Martin Luther King and Roy Wilkins, were attacked for the same thing. There was no more vociferous critic of King than Malcolm X for King's relationship with the Kennedys and Johnson.

I think Obama is able to absorb the criticisms without taking them personally. His reaction always seems to be, *I understand the criticism*. I think he believes some of it is ill informed, for instance, from blacks who aren't aware of how some of his policies provide a direct benefit to the black community. But I think he also sees some of it as legitimate, coming from groups frustrated with the pace of change and with their inability to lift themselves out of difficult circumstances. There's also another interesting element to the criticism: A lot of people forget he was a community organizer. He knows the difference between real, legitimate criticism and guys out there just posturing to get on the news. He came out of their world, unlike most high-ranking public officials. This is a man who could have gone into the corporate world and made a huge amount of money but who decided instead to work in Altgeld Gardens in Chicago with poor people. And he has enough African-Americans around him to keep him close to what's happening on the ground, to give him intel on things he doesn't already instinctively know himself. I think that may be part of the problem that many of his critics have; he may be more in touch than they are. He comes out of a different generation from many of them, from a Northern urban setting, the rap, hip-hop generation, not the Southern civil rights, Mahalia Jackson, "Amazing Grace" generation. So on an issue like gay rights, he probably has more of an understanding of shifts in the country and in the black community than many of these guys criticizing him. Many of the black preachers who stood out there and attacked him for his support of same-sex marriage had never criticized a president before. I was flabbergasted. Wait, we forgave senators and presidents for personal immoral acts, prayed for them, went to the White House and slobbered all over them and anointed them with oil. Now Obama takes a personal position, and you're telling people not to vote, while you never did that against people who committed acts that personally we felt were wrong? Come on, are you kidding me? Just tell the truth—say you don't agree with him or you don't like him or some Republicans gave you some money to attack him. But don't act as if you're going to dictate the actions of the rest of us.

In November 2012, we got clear and irrefutable evidence that Obama understood the community more than his critics did. Despite the attacks and the predicted fall-off in his black support, he got a huge turnout of black voters—in many states, more than in '08. Not only did blacks come out to vote, but they stood in line for five or six hours to do it in some places. So at the end of the day, whom were the critics speaking for? What happened to all their threats? In the end, it appears that perhaps he understood more than they understood.

There's no constituency group I'm aware of that doesn't think the president could do more for them. Latinos ask why they didn't get the DREAM Act passed. The gay community asks why it took so long for him to support same-sex marriage, which he was not in favor of at the beginning of his administration. Everybody wants more. That's the burden of the world's biggest job.

As we look upon Obama's second term, the black, Latino, union, gay, and progressive white communities need to understand that we are under siege. Even as the election showed that the country is changing and that we have more electoral power than ever before, that's not reflected in the country's policy-making right now. At last count, twenty-four states were considering right-to-work laws that could push unions into extinction. The Voting Rights Act was gutted by the Supreme Court when they removed Section 4 and it became a rallying cry for our 50th Anniversary National Action to Realize the Dream March on Washington. Several so-called swing states are considering changing their electoral college process from winner-take-all to proportional representation based on congressional districts—meaning a Republican presidential candidate could overwhelmingly lose the state's popular vote but walk away with a majority of the electoral votes. *Roe v. Wade* is one case away from being squashed by the Supreme Court.

If the progressive community does not use the next four years under Obama to legislatively, and with executive action if necessary, cement what we have achieved, we will find ourselves in a very bad state. We must push Obama to help us salvage what we have already achieved in the civil rights movement, the women's movement, and the gay rights movement. Otherwise, the next president will be looking at a land-scape that resembles 1950s America. We must activate every resource we have—from mass marches to boycotts to petition drives—to come together. We must use technology, too, as in recent movements around the world. The president can be a major ally as we undertake this—but only if we don't waste a lot of time indulging our egos and making him the enemy. If we get caught up in the pettiness, I fear we will look back in twenty years and wonder why we didn't take advantage of so many opportunities to get more done when he was in office. And while we look back with regret, our grandchildren by law will not even have the rights and legal protections we have. What a sad day that would be.

As for me, I'm not going to be bogged down in the mire of people condemning me for having access to the White House. After all, as I said before, other black leaders before me didn't let such critiques keep them from pushing forward, so I must do the same. There's never been a day in our history when every black leader agreed on everything—proving total unanimity isn't necessary to get things done. Complete unity and harmony would be wonderful, but it wouldn't be wise for me to waste time and energy yearning for something that we've never had before.

And none of us should forget the importance of asking for what we want, whether from the president of the United States or from a spouse sitting across the table. Not the president, not our boss, not even our loved ones can read our minds.

19

A TRUE LEADER HAS TO BE DISCIPLINED—AND CONSISTENT

It wasn't until I was well into adulthood that I connected my obesity to the traumas I experienced when I was a child. Before that moment of introspection, I had a list of rationalizations that I would wield like a nimble flyswatter, batting away any questions or ridicule connected to my weight.

Oh, they just don't understand black church culture . . .

Black preachers are supposed to be overweight—it makes the congregation more comfortable . . .

What, am I going to be rude and turn down all the meals I get offered as a leader of the black church?

In other words, I didn't see my weight as a problem. It was just a part of me, one of the essential elements of Al Sharpton, minister and civil rights leader.

Anyone who is familiar with the black church knows that the church world is based first on a solid bedrock of God. And not far behind is food. Eating soul food, eating all the wrong foods in terms of a healthy diet, was the norm. I'm talking about fried chicken three times a day—in the morning with grits and eggs for breakfast, a fried chicken sandwich for lunch in the afternoon, and half a chicken at night for dinner.

When I started getting heavy as a youngster, I didn't have to worry about standing out. As I said, in the world of the black church, being heavy was not uncommon; in fact, it was almost expected, particularly among ministers. Most of the ministers I saw were large, to the point where if they weren't, people would think they were unhealthy. The pride of many church folk was to have the minister come eat at their house, where they would keep heaping food on his plate. As I moved through my teens and became more well known, preaching at churches all over the Northeast, I started getting those dinner invitations. People were constantly feeding me, and it certainly was not proper to turn the invitations down. And when you sat down at their table, you couldn't tell them to stop piling on the food—not as if I would have wanted them to stop, anyway. In my spare time, I began hanging out with other preachers, men who had no discipline at all about eating.

It only got worse—much worse—when I went out on the road with James Brown when I was eighteen. For those of you who have never done any extensive traveling with a musician, let me draw a picture of life on the road with the Godfather of Soul. You're literally going from plane to hotel to venue to hotel to plane, and then you do the same thing over again the next day. When you come back to the hotel at about midnight after the performance, you order room service—probably something fried, with lots of starches—and then you go to bed on a full stomach. Remember, this was in the early '70s. Hotels didn't even have fitness centers yet, if you were inclined to try to get in a workout. But doing a workout never crossed my mind, anyway.

One day I woke up, and I was 300 pounds.

Well, that's what I'm guessing I weighed—I didn't take any kind of self-inventory that would involve getting on a scale. In fact, nearly two decades would pass before I actually got on a scale. When I got stabbed in Bensonhurst in 1991, they weighed me in the hospital, and I was more than 300 pounds.

Starting in my teen years, I was in the bubble of the church world and the entertainment world, spending all my time with friends or church folk, so even the women I was going to date or eventually marry came out of a small circle that was preordained. There was nothing to make me look at myself critically or even to think about the big belly I was carrying around.

But one day, when my daughter Ashley was about five, she looked up at me with the innocent, curious eyes of a child and asked, "Daddy, why are you so fat?"

Suddenly, faced with a simple enough question from my child, all those black-church rationalizations sounded silly. In that moment, I began my long journey to become a living embodiment of the things I preached: the need for personal discipline and to hold human life in high regard, which, for me, started with prioritizing my personal health.

When I became a mainstream figure in New York in the 1980s, my weight was one of the first things that people would use to parody me. I was quite the compelling target, with the sweat suits and medallions and long, flowing, pressed hair. But despite the cartoonish depictions that would appear in tabloids such as the *New York Post*—even a memorable front-page picture in the *Post* showing me in the chair at the beauty salon with rollers in my hair—I still wasn't bothered by the mocking. I was still a product of that black-church bubble, still spent most of my time with church folk and religious leaders, so it was easy to dismiss it all. Even when a lot of my friends started becoming health-conscious, I would just tell myself that was part of their idiosyncrasies. Some people smoked; they ate healthy food.

But then came those fateful words from my daughter, asking me why I was so fat. And I started looking inward, asking myself some tough questions. What answer could I give a five-year-old that would make sense? I couldn't tell her she just didn't understand church culture, or, even worse, would I be inadvertently resigning her to an obese future, since church culture was her culture, too? How could I tell her that? At that moment, I began to wonder, *Wait a minute, what am I projecting to my kids?* I spent much of my life looking for a father figure. Now I was the father figure for my girls—what image was I giving them?

Those questions stunned me. I had never stopped to think about these things before, had never considered the entirety of the image I was projecting to the world. *Am I that reckless, both in terms of language and appearance?* I started to reevaluate what I wanted to look like, what I wanted to project and say to the world. So I went back to the books.

Dr. King and Nelson Mandela were devoted to discipline. They saw leadership not as something that was segmented, compartmentalized in a specific slot of their lives—which is what I had been doing, in a sense—but as something that needed to run through every aspect of their lives. Mandela was a boxer, an athlete who maintained his health so well during his twenty-seven years in prison that he was able to walk out of there erect and in great shape, and he remained vibrant well into his nineties. Dr. King wrestled with his weight—no doubt from being ensconced in the church world—but he would never let himself get out of control with it.

And just as important, both of them thought a lot about the temperament of leadership, controlling your mind and your mouth, in addition to your body. I had put in many sacrifices, had my life endangered by being stabbed, had been getting attacked for many years, but I still hadn't given enough attention to the temperament of leadership, the rhetorical discipline. It dawned on me, reading about these great men, that if I wanted to go to the next level, I needed to take control of my mouth—both what I put into it and what I allowed to come out of it. What I ate and what I said. And I could only do that by controlling my mind, controlling my appetites. To me, that became the path to greatness; it was the only way I could go from being a famous leader to being a great leader.

While I thought compartmentalizing was working for me,

this time of study and introspection revealed to me that it wasn't working. We're all one person. We may have many facets to our personalities, but I saw that they are all connected. The image you project publicly and the way you treat yourself—it's all tied together.

This message started to find its way into my sermons and the words I was delivering to the black community. I began to preach about the need to be consistent and disciplined in all aspects of our lives. You can't preach about the abundant life and then tell people to go downstairs into the church cafeteria and kill themselves. In effect, to dig their graves with their teeth. This transformation made me think more deeply about the way food dominated the black church community and even to think more analytically about the food itself. For example, what we call soul food came out of a slave culture. We had to eat heavy meals because we worked in the fields all day and night. So when you're working in the fields from sun-up to can't-see, doing grueling manual labor, you not only need to eat certain foods to give you strength, but you will sweat away thousands of calories every day. Now most of us spend our days behind a laptop in an office. Clearly, that can't be compared to working in the cotton fields in Alabama. So the diet our great-grandmothers and great-grandfathers needed to survive in the fields, probably burning upward of 3,000 to 4,000 calories a day, is totally inappropriate today, completely antithetical to our dietary needs when we work behind a desk, burning next to nothing.

We're no longer slaves. I preach a sermon based on

Galatians 4, where Paul is trying to advise the Galatians to stop acting as if they are still in slavery. Black people are corporate CEOs now, governors, even president of the United States—so why do you still have a slave diet? African-Americans would be quick to attack someone who spoke to us as slaves—but then, when it's time to eat, please hand me the slave lunch menu. Either we are the twenty-first-century children of those who rose to the unbelievable levels we have achieved, with everything from the menus to the habits and social life that goes with our status, or we are not. You can't go backward and forward at the same time. These are the thoughts I had to come to terms with as I did an inventory on my life, my thinking, and my diet.

This is one of the great challenges for the black community and the black church—and also for the Latino community and poor Southern whites, too—if we are going to rise up and fight against people looking at us as if we are nothing and treating us as if our lives are without worth. If we are going to battle to insist that our lives have merit, have value, then how are we going to proceed to kill ourselves with our own diet?

The basic fact underlying all my work is that every human life has value. But how can I preach the value of human life and at the same time preach that it doesn't matter what you do to your human life with your diet? I knew I couldn't have it both ways. You can't say it's all right to kill yourself with diabetes and hypertension and high blood pressure and obesity but still parade around telling everyone to value all human life. If you value life, you have to value it in all ways. At least, that's what

I came to believe about my own life. So that made me act to take control of my diet.

Over the past couple of years, I've gotten an endless number of requests from magazines and periodicals asking me for the specifics of my diet, but what worked for me may not work for everybody. I came up with a plan by doing a lot of research, talking to doctors, and learning how my body works. I'll give the basic outlines here, but by all means, don't consider this a diet guide.

I don't eat any meats. I eat fish maybe twice a week. Mostly, I eat salads and uncooked fruit and some whole-wheat toast which provides some grains and starch to give me sustenance for the exercise I try to do every morning. At first, I didn't do the toast, but my doctor told me that if I was going to do the treadmill, I needed to have something substantial in my stomach. So I'll eat some whole-wheat toast in the morning and maybe at night. Other than that, we're talking fruits and salads and fish—but the fish is most likely on the weekends.

It took me about a year to lose the first hundred pounds. A rate of two pounds a week is about as fast as you want to go with weight loss. The people around me at first were startled. I used to be the kind of guy who ate all the time, big meals, heaping servings. That was something you could count on with Rev. Al Sharpton. When people realized this was something I was serious about, they began to get a little uncomfortable eating around me. I would tell them it didn't bother me, but people were still self-conscious about sitting there with a heaping plate full of things I used to covet, while

I ate my salad. Eventually, they got over it. In the church and civil rights communities, people thought I was sick, which was understandable. There would be whisper campaigns: "What's really wrong with him? Why's he losing all that weight? Come on, tell me if something is wrong with him—I don't want to read about it in the newspaper." A couple of people actually worked up the nerve to ask me, "You all right, Rev?"

One morning, during one of our weekly Saturday rallies in Harlem, I said on the radio: "What's been interesting to me as I've lost the weight is that when I was 300 pounds and obese, nobody asked me, 'Are you all right?' When I got healthy, everybody asked, 'Are you all right?' You should have been asking me that a year ago, when I was killing myself!" But it's a consequence of the culture of obesity we're dealing with in the country as a whole and particularly in the African-American community. A child is much more likely to hear, "Boy, sit down and eat—you don't look healthy." Really? You're not looking healthy because you're not overweight, not obese?

I've heard people actually say that I lost weight because I got a television show on MSNBC. But I had already taken control of my diet before I got the TV show. I acknowledge that many celebrities lose weight because they're concerned about their public image, but my motivation was to personify what I believed and what I was teaching. It had nothing to do with the public. In fact, I never really thought about how the public was going to react. There have been other changes I have had to make as a result of my weight loss that I also hadn't calculated, such as the impact it would have on my wardrobe. People see me wearing these fancy suits on television and say, "Ooh, look at Sharpton, wearing the fancy Italian suits now that he's on television!" But in reality, I had to buy a whole new wardrobe because I couldn't wear the suits I used to wear. So when you restock your wardrobe and you have a few dollars in your pocket, you're going to buy what's in style. It has nothing to do with a television show; it's just a practicality. If I wore one of my old suits on television, my shoulders would be down at my elbows.

I was already separated when I started losing weight, so that meant I was out on the dating market as the pounds were dropping off. I think at some point, I got caught up in the stereotypical middle-aged male mind-set—an old man dating young girls to try to affirm himself, prove he is still young and vital. But then I told myself, *You need to stop this, What are you trying to prove?* I knew I needed to settle down again. Carrying around those middle-age insecurities, needing a young woman to tell me I was still a man, all of that was antithetical to having a serious contribution to make in my life. From your diet to your friends to your social life, you have to say either you're going to be serious about leadership in all aspects or you're not going to be serious.

I've lived long enough to see with so many leaders that if you start living a life of contradictions, your enemies can use it against you. Even if you never get caught, the contradictions weigh down on your ability to be effective because you know you're living a double life. It's not even necessary for you to be a CIA director like Gen. David Petraeus; you can just be a regular guy with a wife and a family. I knew it was going to help me as a man and as a leader to be whatever it is I'm preaching. And you have to be able to withstand the self-inventory if you're going to seek greatness. I don't think in any way that I've achieved greatness, but I have to be honest and admit that greatness is what I seek.

It's an admission we shouldn't shy away from—that we want to achieve greatness. People might say, "Oh, but that's vain." But Martin Luther King said we all have a drum-major instinct. He didn't say we have a want-to-be-in-the-band instinct. He said drum major, the man or woman who's out there in front, leading the show. That's where we want to be. You can certainly see that in the reality-show craze sweeping the globe. It's a response to the human drum-major instinct. So, King said, if you're already trying to be out front, pushing to be the drum major, then why don't you be a drum major for justice? If you're going to be out front, then you have to accept the responsibilities that go along with that. For my life, the full interpretation was, even though you're a celebrity, you can't date just anybody anymore. And you can't eat just anything you want and look any old way anymore. And you have to consider what comes out of your mouth. And when that guy takes shots at you, you're going to have to refrain from shooting back, because you represent a higher cause than yourself. You can't aspire to be the drum major of a band but live by the rules of the regular band members. If you want to live by the rules of a band member, then you should just step back and be a regular member of the band.

If you're going to be a drum major, if you're going to be a front man, if you're going to be a leader of your family, of your community, of your people, then there are different rules that you have to live by. I have accepted my role as a drum major, and I try every day to be as consistent as possible about the image and the message I project to the world. If I'm going to preach and protest whenever I see human life being disrespected and denigrated, then I must show the ultimate respect for my own life by demonstrating concern for my health.

And even though I'm not getting any younger, I have a confession to make: I feel great.

20

EVERY LIFE HAS VALUE

The notion underlying most of the fights I have engaged in as a civil rights leader over the years is that every life has value. It is an idea fundamental to Christianity and to human rights. But I was never more stunned at how easily lives can be devalued and rendered cheap than when I went to Rwanda in 1994.

I felt African-American leadership should be doing more at the time to challenge the Clinton administration to intervene in the massacre that ultimately resulted in as many as a million Tutsis—nearly 20 percent of the Rwandan population—being slaughtered by Hutus. On our trip to Rwanda, we first stayed in Goma, Zaire—now the Democratic Republic of Congo—and drove two hours across the border to Kigali, the capital city of Rwanda. Every two or three miles, we would be stopped by these unbelievably young kids, fourteen- or fifteen-year-olds, brandishing automatic weapons and demanding to search our car to see if we were hiding any Hutus. The guys in my delegation were shaken by the danger of the situation, but I kept thinking, *How are these kids who barely have clothes to wear getting automatic weapons? Who is arming this tribal war?*

Rwanda is so breathtakingly beautiful, as if you have stepped onto the most fertile, gorgeous land that God ever created; it looked as if you could spit on the ground and a tree would grow. But once you thought about the sights we were coming across, it was obvious that the forces of big business and transcontinental corporations that were exploiting the mineral resources of Rwanda—and many other African countries— were financing these tribal wars, arming the countryside, because as long as there's chaos, they can manipulate the land and the minerals. So, heartbreakingly, you get people in these countries fed by greed and a hunger for power, driven by a total disregard for the worth of human life, who fall right into the trap, walking into villages and not thinking twice about killing an entire family, just because they are in a different tribe. I saw this with my own eyes—families and villages wiped out. Annihilated. There was no recognition that each one of those people had value—they were seen as representations of tribes, Hutus or Tutsis, not individual men, women, and children who could make a valuable contribution to mankind. One of those children who were slaughtered could have been the scientist who develops the ultimate cure for cancer or the next great African musician or athlete or political leader. All of that human potential, just wiped off the face of the earth. And it wasn't potential that might have benefited only Africans or people of color—each of those lives could have had value for all of mankind, no matter what complexion or country of origin. A great musician, doctor, scientist, or politician can have an impact far beyond his own people or her own country.

I came home thinking about how easily Americans detach ourselves from the rest of the world, romanticizing our relationship with our homeland—whether African-Americans, Italian-Americans, Irish-Americans, and so on—but not doing a thing actually to help the people still living in these countries. It's a sort of mindless boasting—"I'm Irish," "I'm Italian," "I'm African-American"—and we pay lip service to the importance of our ancestors and our lineage. But how many of us take the next step and go back to our countries of origin to offer assistance, to make sure the citizens are thriving and able to sustain themselves? If I'm Irish, I should be concerned about the state of the economy in Ireland and the lack of jobs and opportunity. If I'm African-American, I should care that they slaughtered a million Rwandans or that there is slavery in the Sudan. How do you find pride in something but not be proud enough to preserve the integrity of that thing that brings you pride?

The painful lessons of intragroup hostilities also came up during my memorable meeting with Fidel Castro in Havana. I was in Jamaica for a gathering of Caribbean newspaper publishers in Montego Bay in 2000, and I was going to be flying over to Havana with several members of the U.S. Congress who were on the trip. But when they got called back to Washington for a surprise session of Congress, the Cuba jaunt was called off. But I still wanted to see Cuba, so I asked one of my assistants to see if he could get us there anyway. It turned out that I was allowed to go on a religious visa.

So I got onto a plane with three others from my group, and we landed in Havana, where they immediately took us to the Hotel Presidente and put us up in very nice suites. Right away, I put in a request to meet with President Fidel Castro. The officials who were minding us looked a bit skeptical, but they said they would try. We went to an international gathering of Communist leaders at the Karl Marx Auditorium. We saw Daniel Ortega, the former Nicaraguan president whom Ronald Reagan had been trying to overthrow in the Iran-contra scandal. We sat there for hours, watching the proceedings. The next day, we went back, and it was the same thing, sitting in that auditorium for hours. I was supposed to be leaving the next morning, so I figured the meeting with Castro was not going to happen. That evening, I was sitting out in the plaza of the hotel, listening to the group of musicians who walked around to entertain the tourists. A stranger came over to me and told me that I was to go to the convention center again the next morning before my three P.M. flight, but I should bring all of my luggage with me, because I was going to meet Castro on the way to the airport.

"But you cannot tell anyone traveling with you," he cautioned me, which I thought was odd. He walked away without another word.

Next, I had a meeting with Rev. Lucius Walker, the progressive activist preacher who had started a group called Pastors for

Peace, which focused on battling American imperialism abroad, fighting issues such as the trade embargo of Cuba and American policies in Latin America. Walker had been to Cuba many times to meet with Castro, so he briefed me on the protocol of such a meeting and once again warned me about telling the rest of my group about the meeting.

When we left the next morning, the guys in my group couldn't understand why I made them bring all their luggage when we weren't leaving until later in the day. We sat in the Karl Marx Auditorium for the third day in a row. But after about ninety minutes, a Cuban official came to get us and rushed us to a van, which drove us about a half hour to a modern building. We walked in and got into the elevator, which took us up to the second floor. When the doors opened, there was Fidel Castro, standing with his hands extended. I could hear the audible gasps of my delegation; they were stunned.

"I always wanted to meet you," Fidel said to me.

After that, he spoke to me in Spanish through an interpreter. Over lunch, we talked about the ongoing election drama in the United States between George Bush and Al Gore. This was in November 2000, when Florida was counting ballots and the nation was fascinated by the specter of the "hanging chad." Well, Fidel was fascinated, too. Clearly, the outcome of the election would have a significant impact on him and his nation—one can easily imagine that the last decade of Cuban life and politics would have looked much different if Gore had won. Fidel asked me who I wanted to win, Gore or Bush, although I'm sure he already knew my answer. I told him what the election tally looked like when we had left the States, but he had more up-to-date numbers from the previous hour, which he shared with me. That's how closely he was watching the proceedings. He told me he was familiar with all my work on racial issues in America.

"We have the problem of race here in Cuba," he stated.

"Really?" I asked, surprised that he would go there.

"I can bring you down to Santiago, where I grew up," he said through the interpreter. "It's mostly black people, and the people my complexion look down on them, even now under my rule. We have a problem of race all over the world."

I was shocked to hear this from the world's most famous Communist leader, an acknowledgment that his country was still fighting the evils of racism and colorism. But it reminded me that tribalism, classism, racism, and colorism are international problems, affecting humans in virtually every corner of the globe. In America, we need to move beyond a parochial view of African-American discrimination and start thinking about forming a global coalition. As a human rights activist, just as I am committed to fighting discrimination against gays and immigrants, I know I need to expand my perspective to fight against all discrimination, whether it's Hutus against Tutsis, sexism and misogyny across the globe, or classism in Latin America.

As the most powerful nation in the world, America needs to set an example, to be a beacon for all on how to fight against these -isms that plague the globe, rather than reinforcing their inevitability.

In 2001, I traveled to southern Sudan—which is now a separate nation—to witness with my own eyes something that radio host Joe Madison had told me about: Sudanese people being sold into slavery. We flew into Nairobi, Kenya, where we were met by a group of guys who flew us in a propeller plane into southern Sudan. We had to go up and down four times to refuel and stay as surreptitious as possible, because we weren't supposed to be there. We went out into the bush, where we stayed in a tent for two nights and witnessed the slave trading. I interviewed people on video with a translator, and they told me they were forced to work for nothing and that if they didn't pray the way they were ordered to pray, they would be raped or have a finger cut off. This was black against black, African against African. So unless we have a global standard against tribalism, racism, and classism, our work as human rights activists is not done. Given the technology of today, it's possible to have a global movement. I've spent many hours talking about this with Martin Luther King III, about how the ethic of love and equal justice must be fought for around the world. So on one level, we must work to cement the civil and human rights gains we've made in the past, but on another level, we must move outside the United States to join with these freedom campaigns across the world that we've seen in recent years. Nobody planned the Arab Spring; people demanded it.

Traveling outside of the United States can be an important agent in broadening our perspective about American problems. When Castro confessed that Cuba was struggling with colorism, it made me realize the issue isn't unique to African-Americans, so perhaps we shouldn't be so hard on ourselves. But at the same time, we need to expand the conversation about how to solve these issues by including people of color around the world, in the Caribbean, Africa, and Asia. And while we're at it, we might include white people in the conversation, too, because ultimately, every person on the planet is affected when any of us is kept from reaching his or her potential, regardless of the reason.

21

BEWARE OF THE DANGER
OF EXTREMES

The need to establish relationships outside the borders of the United States and to fight extremism around the world was brought home to every American with undeniable force on September 11, 2001, when my city was devastated by terrorists. I knew people who died in the World Trade Center. As a matter of fact, a young man who went to church with my kids lived with us after he lost his mother in the attack. I watched him every day slowly having to come to terms with the reality that his mother was not coming back. In the first few days, he jumped every time the phone rang, thinking it was his mother or the authorities telling him she had been found in the rubble and she was all right. After about three weeks, he finally started to accept the brutal fact that she was gone. It was heartbreaking. His mother had nothing to do with U.S. foreign policy. She didn't make any decisions about what was going on in Iraq or Afghanistan. But everybody died in those towers—black, white, Latino, Asian, Jew, Arab. If you were in there, you were gone. It was an equal-opportunity devastation. I felt that we needed to make a statement against this recklessness, where people felt they could take the lives of others based on their own extreme beliefs.

When people are faced with instability, whether through economic crashes, military takeovers, or citizen uprisings such as the Arab Spring, they tend to run to extremes. They want to hold on to something that will make them feel empowered, will carry them through the storm, such as military might or religious fundamentalism. I believe that's why we've seen this explosion in fundamentalist escapism in recent years; people want some help in standing on their own two feet. The leaders of these movements play on people's fears and anxieties, rather than teaching them to be fearless and to grow with the changing times. What I've learned in traveling across the United States and the world and meeting with people during their times of trouble is that if you can find a way to endure the storm, it is always going to get better. There's a bright sun on the other side. Don't succumb to hate and militarism as a way to ease the pain. If you give in to the extremes, you won't even know the sun has come out, because you will be too blinded to see it.

After the events of September 11, 2001, I called Mort Zuckerman, the owner and publisher of *U.S. News and World Report* and the *New York Daily News*, who at the time was chairman of the Conference of Presidents of Major American

Jewish Organizations. I told him I wanted to go to Israel. Because I had been a controversial figure in some Jewish circles, I thought it would be a powerful message if I went there to make a statement about how the world must stand together against terrorism, extremism, and the shedding of innocent blood. Zuckerman thought it was a great idea, and he arranged a formal invitation to me from the government of Israel. I would be hosted by Shimon Peres, the minister of foreign affairs at the time who became president of Israel in 2007. On the ten-hour flight to Israel, I saw that I was sitting in first class with Ehud Barak, who had just stepped down from his post as prime minister after losing to Ariel Sharon. I went over to speak with him.

Barak said to me with a laugh, "You know, I was thinking with me and you on the same flight, if the terrorists knew we were up here together—boom!"

The whole rest of the flight, I would jump every time the plane hit a bump, thinking to myself, *Why did he have to joke like that?*

After I landed and we were on our way to the King David Hotel, a car blew up about half a mile in front of us. That was normal life for them; it didn't even seem to be that big a deal, which really exemplified for me the purpose of my visit. I saw all the important sites while I was there—the Holy Land, Calvary where Jesus was crucified, the Wailing Wall, the Holocaust Museum. I met with some of the Ethiopian Jews living there. I also met with many families who had lost family members to terrorism. But while I toured the country, I kept hearing the same message from various Israeli leaders: I needed to go over to the Palestinian side and also talk to them about fighting terrorism. But I was nervous about that, given the sensitivity of the American Jewish community and the knee-jerk tendency of the American media to stir up controversy. I remembered all the trouble Jesse Jackson got in back in '79 when he hugged Yasser Arafat. In the middle of our meeting with Shimon Peres—I was traveling with a mixed delegation of blacks and Jews—Peres also implored me to meet with the Palestinians.

"You should denounce bin Laden and terrorism from the Arab side. You should go to Palestine," he said.

"The right wing in America would distort it if I went over there," I said. "They would say I'm united with the Palestinians."

But Peres dismissed my concerns. "We will tell them we invited you." I still wasn't sure, but then he said, "It's all arranged. You're meeting at one o'clock with Yasser Arafat."

"Huh? How am I doing that?"

"We've arranged it," he repeated. "We've already informed your State Department and Secretary Colin Powell."

I was taken aback quite a bit, but I knew it was best just to go along. Next thing I knew, my delegation was whisked in two vans to the Gaza border. We got out and waited in an office. About twenty-five minutes later, three fancy Mercedes-Benzes sent by Arafat pulled up. As we were getting into the cars, I teased the Israelis: "Arafat has better rides than y'all!"

Right away, we rode through some of the worst squalor I've ever seen, like something out of Dickens. But after about a half hour of driving, we came upon a neighborhood of fabulous beach homes, like spreads you'd see in Beverly Hills or Brentwood, California. We pulled up to a complex of buildings, and I saw about 100 cameramen and reporters thronging outside, waiting for me. I was stunned, wondering how you got together such a mammoth press delegation in the middle of the desert. I waded through the phalanx of journalists up to the second floor, where I saw two wing chairs sitting next to each other, with a couch on the side of each one. They gestured for me to sit in one of the chairs, and my delegation sat on the couch to my right. The Palestinian leaders sat on the other couch, leaving the other wing chair open.

After about ten minutes, French doors swung open, and Yasser Arafat walked into the room, dressed in full regalia. For a moment, I froze, unsure of my next move. If I got up to embrace him, I didn't know if there were cameras in the room that would take the image and blow this whole meeting up. But at the same time, how do you not get up to greet him properly, the head of state in Palestine? Arafat stood there without saying anything, without looking at me, just a statue in the middle of the room. Finally, he sat down in the other wing chair, but he still didn't do anything, and he still hadn't looked at me. Now I was thoroughly confused. *What am I supposed to be doing?* After about a minute—which felt like ten—the French doors swung back open, and suddenly, all the photographers and cameramen appeared. When they were all in position for the shot, Arafat finally reached out his hand toward me. I was stumped again. *Either I shake his hand and the pictures will follow me for a couple of years, or I don't shake it and I've insulted a head of state in his own country—and I don't know that we'll get out of here!* So I reached over and shook his hand. Did you really doubt that I would? Sure enough, the next day's front page of the *New York Post* featured a picture of the two of us embracing. It didn't matter that the Israelis set it up—the *Post* just wanted the salacious story, regardless of the facts.

Once Arafat dismissed the media, we quickly dived into an intense discussion about terrorism. He was vehemently opposed to the actions of Osama bin Laden.

"I denounced what happened in the World Trade Center," he said. "You should tell people I donated blood to the victims. I consider it one of the most horrific acts in the history of mankind. I have rejected bin Laden misusing the Palestinian cause. What he did has nothing to do with Palestine. It had nothing to do with Islam."

I was stunned by how against bin Laden he was. After about fifteen minutes of discussion, Arafat said, "Let's have some lunch," and the French doors swung open again. There was a huge table, where we all sat and dined on an eight-to-twelve-course meal—lentil soup, rice, lamb, chicken, lots of other delicious morsels. I sat facing Arafat; right next to him sat a member of my delegation, Sanford Rubenstein, the prominent Jewish lawyer who had represented, among others, Abner Louima, the Haitian immigrant who had been brutally abused by police in 1997 and who had just won an $8.75-million lawsuit against the city in July. Rubenstein kept asking Arafat about different food items.

Arafat pointed to a garlic dish. "This helps with potency. How old are you?" he asked Sanford.

When Rubenstein told him, Arafat said the dish would help with his virility. I'll never forget that moment—the head of the PLO and this Jewish guy from Brooklyn, talking about how to stay virile. I said to myself, *I guess there really is just one world.*

After we took some more pictures, Arafat gave me a lovely hand-carved replica of the nativity scene in Bethlehem. I was happy to bring it home for my daughters. I asked him if we could go out and make a joint statement condemning terrorism and if he was comfortable saying something about bin Laden.

He said, "Sure!" So with all the press waiting outside, we went down the stairs together. Arafat was one savvy guy. Not only did he know to wait for the cameras to do the handshake earlier, but this time, just as we reached the bottom of the stairs, all of a sudden, he grabbed my arm for support as we were walking out in front of the cameras. So it looked as if we were arm-in-arm as we went outside—and, of course, that's the photo and video that everybody used.

That whole experience with Peres and Arafat taught me a valuable lesson that has stayed with me and guided me over the past decade: Even when on the outside, these two entities look as if they are in vehement opposition, there is still communication between them, and one of the hardest tasks for both sides is to control the extremists in their midst. That is the challenge of our age, whether we're talking about domestic fights in the U.S. Congress, religious conflicts in the United States and abroad, or civil and human rights movements across the globe: how to deal with the extremists and the zealots. It has certainly been a hallmark of President Obama's time in office.

The Israelis and the Palestinians on the outside appeared to be bitter enemies, not able to agree on even the most basic elements of coexistence. But they never stopped talking. They lived on top of each other; they had to communicate. And because they were both focused on their missions, they knew their disagreements weren't personal. It's a crucial concept that all of us must remember: When you're dealing with adversary or friend, don't involve personal emotion. If your purpose is peace, if your purpose is fighting for your people, you can still communicate with your enemy, because the cause is greater than the two of you. Effective leaders are driven by their goals, not by the personalities on either side. If you find yourself getting caught up in personal disputes, it means you don't have an end goal, or you have forgotten it. In Israel, Peres's purpose was the condition of the Israeli people, while Arafat's was the well-being and autonomy of the Palestinians. They could talk to each other all day long, because their efforts to achieve their goals were too big, too grand, to be tripped up by something as petty as personal dislike or animus.

In America, it feels as if our leaders have become captives of petty politics and superficial obsessions. Where are the great leaders with gravity, who could rise above all of the nonsense, the playing to the cheap seats, and really raise significant issues? The world is undergoing rapid change. For the first time in 5,000 years, there's no pharaoh in Egypt, Libya is changed, Syria is changed. We need leaders to deal with all that change in the world, all these places striving and dying for democracy and inclusion, for leaders who can rise above the petty and the personal and keep the big picture in mind. That means putting aside party differences if the well-being of the American people is at stake. That means fighting the extremists in your midst and always keeping open the lines of communication with the other side.

22

TRUE FRIENDS STICK TOGETHER
THROUGH THE GOOD AND THE BAD

Before I fought against the recording industry and its exploitation of hip-hop, I worked closely with the Jackson family on the Victory Tour in 1984. I heard that some of the black concert promoters who had invested in the Jacksons earlier in their careers couldn't get any dates on the tour. I told the Jackson family that they had to give dates to the people who helped make them. Katherine and Joe Jackson agreed. Michael said he would give dates to some of these promoters, but they had to make sure they got the whole community involved—and he told me I needed to go on the road with them, because he didn't trust the promoters to do it.

So with the Victory Tour, my crew coordinated the whole community piece by making sure community organizations in every city got free tickets for the kids and that the venue was hiring black contractors to do things such as food and beverage. Michael also gave scholarships to local kids.

After the tour, Michael and I became very close friends. He leaned on me for counsel, for spiritual guidance, and for friendship, especially when he was going through his most difficult trials. I might get a knock on my door in the middle of the night. I'd open the door, and the most famous entertainer in the world would be standing on my stoop, wanting to talk. That's how Michael was—impulsive, unpredictable, and incredibly private.

I had one of the most surprising and memorable fights of my life against the music industry at Michael's side. It started one night in the summer of 2002 at the Apollo Theater, where Bill Clinton and the Democratic National Committee were having a big fund-raiser. Michael was one of the guest artists, the first time in decades he had returned to the Apollo. I got there late and stood in the back, watching Michael perform one of his songs. As I was about to leave, an assistant traveling with me told me that one of Michael's guys wanted to speak to me. But I had somewhere else to go; I think I had to give a speech. I arranged to come to Michael's hotel later that evening.

So at about eleven thirty that night, I went to the Palace and called up to Michael's room. I sat there in his suite, waiting, and from behind me, I heard, "Sharpton!" Michael always let you know when he was walking into a room. He didn't waste any time telling me what was on his mind.

"These people are trying to take my catalog," he said. "It's racist, and it's wrong!"

"Michael, what are you talking about?" I asked him.

He went on to tell me how he felt that Sony and Tommy Mottola, the president of the company at the time, were trying to take his assets, the vast music catalog—including all of the Beatles' songs—that he co-owned with Sony. I was sitting there watching him get all worked up.

"Michael, you and I go way back, but are you really going to fight this if I get involved?" I asked. "It really is wrong. Historically, they've done this to black *and* white musicians. But I don't want to get out there, and you don't—"

"No, I'm down, and I want to make a show, Reverend Sharpton," he said, interrupting me.

So I told him about visiting James Brown in jail—I knew James was one of his idols. I told him I saw what record companies had done to artists like James over the years, that they treated the artists as property.

"You see yourself as a great artist, and you are, but they see you as property and a money machine—and when you don't make money anymore, they don't care about you and want to take back all their assets," I said.

He was nodding.

"I tell you what. Johnnie Cochran and I are having a music summit in three weeks. There are going to be musicians there, rappers who couldn't get their money, weren't treated right. We're going to address all these issues with the music industry. And piracy and all of that. Why don't you come to that? If you say something public and join us, then I'll believe you're serious."

"I'm gonna be there," he said, nodding enthusiastically.

"OK, Michael," I said.

I gave him the date, but when I walked out of that suite and closed the door behind me, I said to myself that I probably wouldn't hear from Michael for another three years. I didn't even tell Johnnie about it. I didn't tell anybody. And Johnnie and Michael were close, since Johnnie had represented Michael during the trial for the first child-molestation charges.

On the Friday night before the Monday summit, I was at home in Brooklyn when the phone rang.

"Sharpton!" I heard on the other end when I answered. "Where we at in the morning?"

"In the morning? What are you talking about, Michael?"

"I'm here!" he said. "You said to come."

"Michael, the conference is on Monday."

"Oh, I thought it was tomorrow," he said. "I'm here."

"You're where?"

"I'm staying out by the Newark Airport. I'm not at the Palace," he said.

I came up with another idea. "I tell you what, Michael. We have rallies every Saturday morning. I know you don't get up, 'cause you entertainers get up late. But we have rallies broadcast live on the radio. You ought to come by the rally and tell everybody you're going to be there on Monday."

"What's the address?" he said. "I want to be there."

Again, I said to myself, *Yeah, right. Michael won't show*.

So I had other things on my mind the next morning when I got up to the House of Justice on 145th Street in Harlem, a NAN property where we still hold rallies every week that are broadcast on the radio. When I got there, there was press everywhere. I asked my publicist, Rachel Noerdlinger, what was going on.

"Michael put out to the media that he's going to be at the rally," she said.

I shook my head. "Y'all know Michael won't even get up in time!" I said. I looked at her again. "He really said that?"

She nodded. It must have been true, because the place was surrounded by cameras. I went into my office. Normally, we go on the radio at nine A.M., and I speak at ten. About a half hour later, a long black limousine pulled up, and Michael stepped out. I couldn't believe it; he actually came. I was really stunned. I went down to get him; he followed me upstairs to my office. He had his hairstylist with him, and right away, he was in my mirror, styling his hair.

"Michael, we're live on the radio. I got to go out and speak, come on!"

But he wasn't done yet. He never stopped being a perfectionist. It reminded me so much of James Brown. I remembered the nights James would perform three-hour shows, go into the dressing room, wash his hair, put it in rollers, and sit under the hair dryer for forty-five minutes. I'd be sitting there at three in the morning, begging him, "Mr. Brown, we're only going to the hotel, going to sleep, getting up, and flying to the next city. Ain't nobody gonna see you but the guy at the desk at the hotel."

"Rev, if you're going to be a star, you have to look like a star all the time," he'd say. "You always have to look like somebody people would pay to see."

It used to drive me crazy. I was thinking about that as I stood there watching Michael comb out his hair in my mirror, with the crowd outside, waiting.

The typical NAN rallies would be about 200 to 300 people, a mixture of black church folk, black activists, union members, and some hard-core black nationalists who work with us because of shared goals—even though they don't agree with our tactics. I was up on the stage, looking at some of the hard-core nationalists I'd actually heard call Michael a sellout or say Michael was trying to be white, ridiculing him, talking bad about him bleaching his skin.

But when Michael walked up onto that stage, they were all screaming: "Michael!!!"

It was like an instant metamorphosis. I was stunned. I couldn't believe these were the same folks. David Paterson, the future governor, who would come to the rallies, was on the stage with us. The crowd was steadily getting larger, especially after I announced on the radio that Michael Jackson was at the rally and was going to be at the summit. By the time we were done, the crowd had surged to close to 1,000.

I introduced Michael and brought him to the mic. Like any speaker, he started to get a sense of the crowd. He decided he wanted to address the accusations he'd heard over the years that he was a sellout.

"I know I'm black, and I'm proud of who I am," he said.

People in the crowd were literally crying now. This was Michael Jackson, the biggest pop artist in the history of the world, in Harlem at our headquarters, saying he was proud to be black. And then he took a left turn and said, "But Tommy Mottola is a devil."

I knew Mottola, a Bronx guy who had been instrumental in starting the careers of quite a few black musicians and who had been married at one point to Mariah Carey. I had never detected any hints of devilishness, but Michael clearly had a different experience with him.

After he finished his speech, Michael wasn't done. The freedom of fighting back was feeling good to him. He said, "Let's march on Sony today!" The whole thing was surreal to me. Next thing I knew, Michael had rented a tour bus to bring all of us downtown to Sony's headquarters. Even though it was closed on Saturday, it didn't matter, because Michael had seemingly half the nation's news media following him. Everybody in the free world would hear the message Michael was delivering on this day. We wound up in front of the Sony building with Michael leading the chants: "No Justice, No Peace!"

After that scene, Michael stuck around the city for two more days and went to the conference with Johnnie Cochran and me, making his case in front of a huge audience, which is what he wanted.

Over the next few years, Michael and I would talk periodically. When he went through the second trial, he watched the people around him abandon him. I'll never forget one day when he had me visit him at Neverland, which was easily the most beautiful property I've ever seen in my life—the amusement park, the zoo, the ornate rooms, the gorgeous landscaping, a top-notch chef with twenty-four-hour, five-star-restaurant service. I told Michael that if heaven was better than this, then I just had to go. We walked around, and he casually pointed to different locations on the property. "You see that spot over there, Sharpton?" I'd follow his finger, and he'd tell me some huge superstar had gotten married there. "He won't even return my phone calls now," Michael said. Then he'd say he loaned another big star a lot of money at some point, and he couldn't even get the star on the phone.

Almost all the people Michael considered his friends walked away from him when he started fighting Sony, and then they sprinted away from him when he got indicted on the second child-molestation charges. One of the reasons I was and still remain loyal to the Jackson family was the integrity they showed during the trial. Every single day, Michael's parents and all his siblings walked him into that court. I didn't see any of those folks who, after he died, professed how much they loved Michael. Yet the family members these critics all claimed were robbing him were the only people who stood with Michael when everybody thought he was going to jail. At one time, he was the most popular entertainer in the world, but in the end, he wound up all alone except for the people with whom he had started his unbelievable journey.

One day during the trial, I turned on the television, and they were doing a piece on the type of jail cell Michael would be living in after his conviction. It killed me; they convicted the man before the trial was even over. I kept going on the news, saying the man was supposed to be innocent until proven guilty and that I didn't believe the charges and neither

242

did his family. But nobody wanted to hear what I was saying. And then he got acquitted, and the public was shocked. But Michael was broken. He saw how all the people who claimed to love him could so quickly turn on him. He never got over that. He was so disgusted, so shaken, that he left the country and moved to Bahrain.

But his ordeal taught me a memorable lesson about friendship. Just as they say in the marriage vows—to have and to hold, for better or for worse—the same idea should apply to friendship. As I saw with Michael, it is during those times that could undoubtedly be considered "worse" when you most need the support of your true friends. Friendship is easy when things are going well. When you're rolling in cash, you have more friends than you know what to do with. But let the cash dry up, some controversy or challenge enter your life, and the fake ones flee like rats escaping a sinking ship. It was a painful lesson for Michael to learn, but it's a lesson that all of us have probably learned at some point in our lives. It's a lesson that I saw with James Brown. Although he had long been seen as one of the most popular entertainers in the world, when he did three years in prison in the late '80s, I was one of the few people who regularly visited him in jail. I could clearly see the agony and isolation that those years visited upon James.

This is a lesson that all of us should hold close to our hearts, so that we remember it well the next time one of our friends is in trouble. And if it helps you to remember, think about the loneliness and pain of the last days of Michael Jackson, the King of Pop.

23

WHAT IS YOUR LEGACY?

I've found myself preaching the funerals of many famous people. On these occasions, I know I have an elevated platform, because many people will be listening. When I preach a funeral, I'm preaching to the living, not to the deceased. I ask myself, *What elements of the deceased's life can I use to challenge the living to forge a better life?* Because everyone who attends the home-going service has his or her own funeral scheduled; they just don't know the date. So I try to frame the life of the person in the casket in a way that can help the life of those left behind.

When James Brown died, I preached all three of his funerals, on three consecutive days. First, we took him to the Apollo and laid him in state, which was my idea. Then we did a private service in Georgia at the church of one of his daughters, and finally came the public funeral at the James Brown Arena in Augusta. At all three services, I wanted to talk about the improbability of his life—a guy abandoned by both his mother and his father, who went to jail as a kid and then went on to transform this thing we call music. So for the living, every excuse you could conjure up about why you couldn't achieve, James had robbed that from you. He was short when entertainers were supposed to be tall. He was dark-skinned when they were supposed to be light-skinned and have "good" wavy air. He broke every barrier there was for a poor, uneducated, young black boy from Augusta.

I was dealing with an incredible amount of pain, because it was as if I had just lost my father, but I had to push my personal feelings aside and describe to the world his legacy. The last time I saw him was when we were changing the name of the arena. Four weeks later, he was lying in a casket in that same arena. And sitting in the audience with me that day was Michael Jackson.

Two and a half years later, Michael was dead, too.

I was on the air doing my radio show in June 2009, when I saw a news item flash on the bottom of the television screen that I always keep on during the show: "Michael Jackson rushed to the hospital." I got a bit nervous, but I hoped it wasn't something serious. I knew Michael had had his share of health issues.

Joel Katz, one of the biggest entertainment lawyers in the business, called me and said, "Get ready to make a statement."

"Yeah, I just saw they rushed him to the hospital," I said.

"No. He's gone," Joel said. "They're going to announce it in an hour."

"What?" I said, my body starting to go numb.

"He's dead."

"Michael's dead? But Joel, he wasn't even sick. What are you talking about?"

"Al, they're going to try to distort his life, make him a pedophile and a junkie. You should be ready to protect your friend's legacy."

I hung up the phone, the heaviness of the moment starting to pull me down. But I had to push through it. I called Rachel Noerdlinger, who's been the head of communications for NAN and my personal publicist for more than a decade.

"Rachel, Michael's dead. Be ready as soon as they announce it, to announce that I want to do a press conference to talk about his legacy."

I wasn't sure she'd even heard me, she was so broken up, crying into the phone.

"Rachel, please hold it together," I said. "We gotta protect Michael's legacy."

"Where do you want to do it—you want to go to head-quarters?" she asked.

"No, let's do it in front of the Apollo," I said.

So within an hour or two, we were in front of the Apollo Theater, where I talked about what Michael had done for music, for the world. From day one, I felt that it was crucial to protect Michael's legacy. More than anybody, Michael broke down the racial barriers in music. Kids all over the world in places like Japan were not only singing his songs—they did that for other American artists, too—but they were dressing like Michael, they were dancing like Michael. Before Michael, there were Elvis and Sinatra; Michael was American culture's first black equivalent to Elvis. We had black artists who were like Elvis in the black community. But Michael was everybody's Elvis. And I knew I needed to protect that.

When I called the Jackson family, Michael's father, Joe, told me I needed to get out there, because Michael would have wanted me there, so I flew out to Los Angeles as soon as I could. When I landed, I sent a text to the family and told them I was on my way. I got a text back telling me not to go straight to the house but to go to the Shrine Auditorium, where Joe was attending the BET Awards. Before I got there, Joe had made a statement outside the auditorium, introducing a new group, which had upset everybody. I didn't know anything about this, so there I was at the auditorium, sitting in the front row, with Joe Jackson on one side of me and Beyoncé on the other side. I started getting a bunch of text messages, but I ignored them. I was thinking, *People are teasing me because I'm sitting next to Beyoncé*. Finally, I looked down at my phone. "Man, Joe Jackson shouldn't have said that," a text said. Then I got two more saying roughly the same thing.

I leaned over to Joe. "Mr. Jackson, what did you say?" I asked him.

"Oh, man, they all upset 'cause I said we got to continue and I got my own record label," he said in his usual gruff manner. To many observers, his comments sounded callous and insensitive, as if he wasn't giving Michael the proper respect by using the clamor and publicity surrounding Michael's death to introduce a new moneymaking venture.

The next day, I went outside with him to speak to the press and try to clear up the dissension.

Meanwhile, the jockeying to be on the funeral program had already begun. Publicist Ken Sunshine, who handled big stars such as Barbra Streisand and Leonardo DiCaprio but whom I had known for years since he was a young guy working for Mayor David Dinkins, was handling the publicity for the funeral. He was getting all kinds of pressure from every corner. Who was going to sing? Who was going to speak? The family held a meeting to talk about it. Randy Jackson, who was very close to Michael, kept saying to me, "Sharpton, I want you on the program." Everybody had told me they wanted me on the program, but I said, "OK, Randy." The final decision came down to Michael's mother, Katherine Jackson. She said she wanted Martin Luther King's kids to say something, and she wanted me to say something, and they had a couple of people they wanted to sing, and that was it, except for a representative from the Congressional Black Caucus. Of course, when the program was released, everybody went crazy, still pushing to get on the program. But it had been decided by Mrs. Jackson. There wouldn't be any changes to the program after she spoke on it.

Next was the jockeying over tickets. Even though it was to be held at the Staples Center, where the L.A. Lakers play and which has about 20,000 seats, it started to feel like a Michael concert. I had all these people reaching out to me for tickets. I remember teasing Diddy because he asked me for four tickets, which I gave to him. Then I saw his mother at the hotel, and she said, "Rev, can you get me some tickets?" I told her I had just given four tickets to her son. "He didn't give me any of his tickets," she said. I joked that she should have gotten the tickets before Diddy. But it was a big deal, a crazy circus of activity.

On the day, as the hour approached, I sat down with Katherine Jackson at the house and told her, "Mrs. Jackson, it's a great honor that you asked me to be on the program. Since I'm one of the only speakers, is there anything you'd like me to say or not say?"

"Well, no, Reverend Sharpton, Michael and you had your own relationship," she said. "Y'all supported each other, y'all loved each other. Just remember, don't get too far into your own dogma. I'm Jehovah's Witness. And don't get too emotional."

"Yes, ma'am," I said.

I knew her religious tradition didn't include the kind of hollering and screaming that you find at Baptist funerals. I had to pull it back a bit.

As I sat there in the VIP section reserved for the speakers and listened to the comments as the program commenced, I thought to myself, *What am I going to say?* I felt very passionate about the points I needed to make, but I knew I had to keep my passion in check, which was a tall order. When my time came, I walked up to the platform and gazed down at the gold casket that contained this man I'd known for almost forty years, and I started talking about the meaning and importance of Michael Jackson.

"When Michael started, it was a different world," I said. "But because Michael kept going, because he didn't accept limitations, because he refused to let people decide his boundaries, he opened up the whole world. In the music world, he put on one glove, pulled his pants up, and broke down the color curtain, to where our videos are shown, where magazines put us on the cover. It was Michael Jackson that brought blacks and whites, Asians and Latinos, together. It was Michael Jackson that made us sing 'We Are the World' and 'Feed the Hungry' long before Live Aid."

The audience was into it now, clapping enthusiastically. I looked down at Mrs. Jackson out of the corner of my eye and saw that she was clapping, too. So I thought to myself, *Let me push the envelope a little more*. I raised it up an octave or so. I didn't want to go further over my time; everyone was only supposed to have three or four minutes, and I was already past six minutes.

I connected Michael's brilliance in making kids across America and across the world comfortable with a black idol, which made them comfortable watching Oprah on television a few years later and comfortable rooting for Tiger Woods on the golf course.

"Those young kids grew up from being teenage, comfortable young fans of Michael, to being forty years old, comfortable to vote for a person of color to be president of the United States," I said. "Michael did that."

The crowd was roaring now, fully in the moment. As I looked down at his family and talked about the pain they all must be feeling, I decided at that moment that I wanted to say something to his children. I knew if it was me in that box—and one day, it will be—I'd want somebody to say something to my kids. I had been monitoring some of the coverage over the previous three or four days, all the disrespectful "Jacko freako" stuff. I needed to say something to those children as someone who knew their father well.

"I want his three children to know, wasn't nothing strange about your daddy—it was strange what your daddy had to deal with," I said.

The crowd stood and cheered at the sentiment. Even his mother and his siblings and his children stood up. What I was talking about was all the fighting Michael had to do—how he had to fight to keep his catalog, how the record companies used to run up crazy bills and try to charge them against him. That was strange. It was strange to open doors for people and have those same people turn around and slam the same doors in your face. That was strange. They talked about him being weird—well, what was weird was that he would outsell everybody, outperform everybody, and still they wouldn't give him his proper credit. I wanted his kids to understand that.

When the whole place stood up, cheering, I was a bit taken aback. I was thinking, *Wow, what do I do now?* I looked down at his daughter, who had jumped out of her chair, clapping, and I thought, *I might as well go all the way now.* So for the next two minutes, I went ahead and did what Al Sharpton does.

"Some came today, Mrs. Jackson, to say good-bye to Michael. I came to say, thank you. Thank you because you never stopped. Thank you because you never gave up. Thank you because you never gave out. Thank you because you tore down divisions. Thank you because you eradicated barriers. Thank you because you gave us hope. Thank you, Michael. Thank you, Michael."

At the repast, Mrs. Jackson thanked me for everything. After I left and went back to New York, I made sure to stay in touch with the family.

Randy called me about two weeks later and asked, "Are you coming to the burial?"

"I thought there were only two hundred invited guests," I said.

"Of course, you're one of the two hundred," he said.

So I flew out again. At the burial, I was sitting there at this mausoleum with the Hollywood elite—Elizabeth Taylor over here, Berry Gordy over there. An hour passed, and still no family, no body. Just a restless crowd of bigwigs, not used to waiting. But for Michael, we all waited. Finally, after an hour and a half, a hearse pulled up, with the family behind it in limos. The ushers escorted Mr. and Mrs. Jackson to the front row, followed by Janet, Jermaine, and all the rest of the brothers and sisters. I was in about the seventh row, waiting for the service to start. The head usher walked over to me and said, "Mrs. Jackson would like to speak to you."

"Now? The service is about to start," I said.

He shrugged. "She said to get you," he said.

So I made my way down the aisle to the front row, where I knelt down next to Mrs. Jackson. "Is everything all right?" I asked her.

"Oh, yes, I'm fine," she said. "We wanted to talk to you for a minute."

Mr. Jackson chimed in. "Al, we want you to say some words for Michael here tonight," he said.

"Now?" I asked, clearly surprised.

"Yeah," he responded with a nod.

Mrs. Jackson put her hand on my wrist. "I want you to do the eulogy," she said. "And I want you to tell the truth for my son."

I was moved by the request. "All right," I said quietly.

I went back to my seat, my mind racing. Gladys Knight got up and sang a beautiful song. Then they announced that I would be doing the eulogy. The people who were sitting with me turned to me in surprise, asking why I hadn't told them I was doing the eulogy. I didn't even have time to tell them that I didn't know I was doing the eulogy until a few minutes earlier.

I got up and walked to the stage. I preached for about twenty minutes on what Michael meant to us and to the world. But I felt I needed to get a bit more pointed at the end. I looked out at the crowd and wondered aloud how many of those out there crying wouldn't even return Michael's phone calls before he died. I recounted how Michael walked me around Neverland, showing me where certain celebrities had gotten married, where others had big social events, and how broken up he was that people wouldn't return his calls after the molestation charges and the fight against Sony. I said to let the lesson be that greatness is not determined by what you are challenged with; greatness is that you can be great no matter what your challenges are. It's not what you go through; it's what you get through. And you should never be disloyal to a great person who was loyal to you.

After I was done, we said a prayer and took Michael's body into the mausoleum. As we placed the body, Gladys Knight sang a breathtaking version of "His Eye Is on the Sparrow." I've never heard anybody sing it like that—if there is such a thing as the voice of an angel, Gladys was as close to it that night as I've ever heard in my life. One of the images that is still with me is of his daughter, Paris, holding her aunt Janet's hand as she watched them place her father's body in the mausoleum.

When I was leaving the cemetery that night—it was past eight P.M., so it was now dark outside—heading toward the repast at a restaurant, a very famous artist stopped me on the way out. I won't give his name, but he's a huge star. He said, "Reverend Al, man, I was so moved by that eulogy!"

"Thank you," I said.

"If I go first, I want you to do my eulogy—and I want you to do it just like that," he said.

I looked at him, and before I could stop myself, I said, "You're gonna have to give me something to work with."

His head dropped, and he walked away.

Most of us don't spend much time considering what they're going to say at our funerals. Over the last few years, I have been warning in many of my sermons that you shouldn't make some preacher have to get up there and hallucinate a life for you that you never lived. At least, leave something that the minister can talk about, something of value that you did, that you stood for, that will be worthy of people remembering you by. If all your life has been geared toward what you own, what you bought, your fun, your games, your trips, just know that all that was for you. It'll all die with you. There was a time when I would get called when somebody died, and I'd be there, ready to stand up and say something nice at the eulogy. But I won't do it anymore. Now, unless I can get up and honestly say something meaningful, I'll pass. I refuse to get up and lie about people just because they died. We're all going to die, and we all should live knowing that death is certain. What's uncertain is life.

What do I want them to say about me when my day arrives?

Yes, I like to live comfortably. Yes, I like being well known. But is that all I want? Is that all I am? Absolutely not. That's no legacy. When my day comes and my funeral is at hand, I want them to say that when the challenges of social justice and economic inequality and racial discrimination were still prevalent, still suffocating the land, Al Sharpton was on the front line, fighting, battling—even if it cost him, even if it was uncomfortable. He was one of the proud soldiers for justice, a rejected stone that God used to be part of a cornerstone of a new world order.

I don't want to be remembered as a TV host, or a radio host, or a big-time preacher, or the head of a civil rights organization. I want people to know that I was somebody who should never have been where I ended up being, according to the norms of the society I lived in. Because there is a special place for rejects God can use. I want my legacy to include the message that I stood up and represented the rejects, that I helped to change the times I lived in. Of course, I didn't do this by myself but with others—some more famous, some less famous. This is the legacy I covet. Others might want to be remembered as the richest guy or the most fashionable guy, but that's not for me. It's important to know what you want your legacy to be, because it directs your steps, blazes your path. And you're going to be dead a lot longer than you're going to be alive.

If you can leave behind a legacy of selflessness, of grace, of advocating on behalf of the weak and the powerless, I guarantee memories of you will far exceed your time here on earth. That's the power of legacies. With all of the ups and downs, the good days and the bad, the pain and the joy, I don't think it should end when they lower you into the ground or scatter your ashes. Your time here should all have been for a reason greater than yourself. I want people years from now, decades from now, to have gotten some meaning out of what I did. Your legacy cannot, should not, be measured by material things. If I had the best car in New York when I died, it will be out of style five years after I die. If I had the biggest house when I died, somebody will soon come along and build a bigger one. But if I make a lasting contribution to advancing humanity and breaking down barriers, changing the social order, people will still be referring to my life's work many years after I'm gone.

Frederick Douglass will be remembered far longer than the richest black man during Reconstruction. Martin Luther King is remembered more than anybody who had a bigger church than he had in the '60s. I believe people need to live for a higher purpose than themselves. Be comfortable if you can, but your goal should be becoming comfortable enough to do great things. The goal shouldn't be the comfort itself. What will it all mean 100 years from now? Will you have been part of something that mattered? Otherwise, you're doing it all for nothing—for some choir to sing "Nearer, My God, to Thee" as your casket is carried out, and that's it. You're forgotten by the time the last car pulls away from the cemetery, because it was all done for some minute, selfish reasons. The desolation of the forgotten. That's not a legacy worth living for. We all should strive to leave behind something greater than ourselves. Fighting injustice. Battling for the dispossessed and powerless. Comforting the afflicted and afflicting the comfortable. Selflessly giving ourselves to those in need. Those are the kinds of words we should all seek to have carved into our tombstones.

If that all sounds too grand for you, if you lean more toward humility, try this one on for size: He made this world a better place.

ACKNOWLEDGMENTS

My sincerest thanks go to the National Action Network (NAN), which allowed me to work on this book while continuing to be president and spokesman for the organization, starting with our chairman, Rev. Dr. W. Franklyn Richardson, and our committed board members, including Vice Chairman Donald Coleman, Lamell McMorris, Rev. Frederick D. Haynes III, Rev. Michael A. Walrond Jr., and the more than twenty other board members who represent NAN.

Thanks to NAN's national staff, chapter leaders, and members, who do the work every day whether they get public recognition or not, headed by Executive Director Tamika Mallory and Executive Vice President and General Counsel Michael A. Hardy, who helped me co-found the organization and who has been a close friend.

I want to thank Nick Chiles not only for using his brilliant skills as a writer to help me in this book but also for being meticulous and extremely careful to preserve my voice, my words, and my message. So what you get is totally from me. He is a brilliant writer, who has immersed himself in a project that is bigger than myself, and I will be eternally grateful for this brother who is truly unique and much appreciated by me.

Thanks to my companion and trusted friend Aisha McShaw, who helped me with this project.

Thanks to Kedar Massenburg, my friend and partner for many years, who is a legend in the music world and our community and who made this book possible and mandatory.

Thanks to Rachel Noerdlinger, who has been with us for more than a dozen years and has done a phenomenal job managing my brand and image.

Thanks to Phil Griffin, who gave me the opportunity to talk to millions as the host of *PoliticsNation* on MSNBC and believed in me, despite criticisms, by helping to democratize the airwaves of cable America. And to Matt Saal, the senior producer of *PoliticsNation*, who has worked with me and bonded with me in an unusual and heartwarming way. And to the staff at *PoliticsNation*, who do the best research and produce the best show on television today.

Thanks to Cathy Hughes and Alfred Liggins, who eight years ago gave me a voice with a daily syndicated radio show and were among the first people to invest in my message and our community. There would not be many of the things that have happened in the twenty-first century for the advancement of human and civil rights without Radio One and TV One, the brainchildren of Cathy Hughes, a black woman unparalleled in American history, and without the development by Alfred Liggins, an unequaled black entrepreneur and communications mogul.

ACKNOWLEDGMENTS

Thanks to Tom Joyner, who has been here for every battle and has given me a weekly voice across America, and to Steve Harvey, who as a radio and television host and author has lent his name and commitment to the betterment of America, and to Ricky Smiley, who follows in the great tradition of black communicators.

Thanks to my best friend and adviser, who has helped keep my focus and helped guide me through my transformation, Dwight McKee, and to many of my partners in progress who work side-by-side with me, along with some younger than I who will continue this long after I am gone, such as Bishop Victor Tyrone Curry in Miami, Rev. Charles Williams in Detroit, Rev. K. W. Tullos in L.A., Mary Pat Hector, head of NAN Youth Move, who reminds me of my National Youth Movement days, and Janaye Ingram, who heads our Washington Bureau office with great diligence, and the list goes on and on.

Thanks to my siblings and family members who have grown closer since the passing of my mother and to Kathy, who did an outstanding job of raising our daughters and remains my friend and supporter.